JEREMY McGRATH

IMAGES OF A SUPERCROSS CHAMPION

KEN FAUGHT

MOTORBOOKS
INTERNATIONAL

To Fay G. Wight, my grandmother, who passed away in 2003. She was the one that convinced my parents to let me have my first motorcycle, a 1976 Indian MX70 given to me by Johnny Posca. She said it would be "a good learning experience," and it most certainly has been a terrific worldly education. Grandma, you'll be forever missed!

First published in 2004 by Motorbooks International, an imprint of MBI Publishing Company, Galtier Plaza, Suite 200, 380 Jackson Street, St. Paul, MN 55101-3885 USA

Motorbooks International titles are also available at discounts in bulk quantity for industrial or sales-promotional use. For details write to Special Sales Manager at Motorbooks International Wholesalers & Distributors, Galtier Plaza, Suite 200, 380 Jackson Street, St. Paul, MN 55101-3885 USA.

ISBN 0-7603-2032-2

On the front cover: McGrath has a unique style of cornering in bowl turns. He actually sits toward the back of his seat and steers with the throttle. *Ken Faught/Dirt Rider*

On the frontis: Jeremy won a record 14 races in the 1996 supercross season, for an average finish of 1.066666th place. *Ken Faught/Dirt Rider*

On the title page: Very few people could ever keep up with McGrath, but Doug Henry managed to give Jeremy a run for his money on several occasions. *Scott Hoffman/Dirt Rider*

On the back cover: Tracy, Ann, Jeremy, and Jack McGrath. *Ken Faught/Dirt Rider*

Edited by Lindsay Hitch and Lee Klancher
Designed by LeAnn Kuhlmann

Printed in China

Contents

Acknowledgments

In 1979 when my dad was out of town on a business trip, a neighborhood kid named Johnny Posca offered to give me a 1976 Indian MX70 dirt bike for free, but I didn't think it would go over well with my parents. I turned to my grandma, Fay Wight, to ask on my behalf. Somehow, she managed to convince my mom it would be a "good learning experience." Little did any of us know the incredible chain of events that would follow.

A few years later, I met Karel Kramer from *Dirt Rider* magazine. He gave me my big break as a test rider, photographer, and journalist. He opened the door, and I ran through it as fast as I could. Along the way, Jack Mangus, Paul Carruthers, Nate Rauba, Kit Palmer, Bryan Catterson, Mark Kariya, Tom Webb, Fran Kuhn, Davey Coombs, Dick Lague, and Fred Koplin helped to guide me throughout my career. I would like to thank each and every one of you for all the support you have given me over the years. I also thank my wife, Amy, and two children, Hannah and Wyatt. You have allowed me to pursue my passion and live life to the fullest. I'm very lucky to be surrounded by good friends and family.

Donnie Bales, Jason Williams, Craig Potter, Steve Lamson, Greg Albertyn, Lee Klancher, Joe Bonnello, and Dick Burleson—you know where you fit in! You guys don't allow me to get caught up in everything and have taught me how to be a better human.

I'm also lucky to have really cool in-laws who support me in everything, and that's difficult with all things considered. Mel Harris, for a guy who only sells a billion dollars worth of motorcycles a year, you're not half bad! Suzuki is lucky to have a leader like you.

I also want to thank Jack, Ann, Tracy, Jeremy, and Kim McGrath. You have given me incredible life experiences, and my world certainly would not be the same without you!

Introduction

On a cold January evening in 1993, Jeremy McGrath scored his first American Motorcyclist Association (AMA) 250cc Supercross win inside California's Anaheim Stadium. The rookie stunned the racing world by acing out the world's fastest riders at one of the most popular venues. I was surprised as well, but it wasn't because of his impressive butt-whooping ride. I was shocked because I knew McGrath as a friend.

I grew up in Southern California, smack dab in the middle of MX Central. Inside my high-school locker, I had pictures of 1980s motocross heroes Rick Johnson, Broc Glover, and Ron Lechien. At home, I had a poster of Roger DeCoster on the wall, and a giant blow-up of the Los Angeles Coliseum. I have been addicted to the sport of off-road motorcycling ever since I was a teenager. To me, the stars of supercross were almost untouchable, but Jeremy's win brought the heroes home for me.

In 1986, Jeremy and I met and quickly became friends. Several times a week after school, I would drive to his parents' muffler shop so we could ride across the street or drive over to their Murrieta, California home to practice in the backyard. The McGraths were like family to me, and now Jeremy had hit it big-time. This was the motorcycle equivalent of remembering playing baseball in the field with a kid who later grows up to be Hank Aaron. This type of stuff is not supposed to happen in real life.

My relationship with Jeremy and his family began when he was an 80cc Novice. As an associate editor of *Cycle News* and now the editor-in-chief of *Dirt Rider* magazine, I have followed Jeremy around the world documenting his incredible success and his rare failures. I've been fortunate enough to know the real Jeremy—the MC who will spend eight hours a day, in the pouring rain, building his own 50 track all by himself; the guy who will show up at a seven-year-old's classroom to be the subject of "show-and-tell"; the guy who set the standard for extreme athletes, and one who's won fans over worldwide.

In reality, Jeremy hasn't changed as much as the people around him have. He's the same fun-loving kid I've known since he was 13; he just happens to have won 72 main events along the way to becoming the greatest supercross racer of all-time. And since his surprise retirement in January 2003, I've been fortunate enough to spend more time with the champ than I did when he was winning. Although his Decade of Dominance has passed, he hasn't lost his passion for riding. In fact, I think he enjoys it now more than ever.

Jeremy managed to suck me into the sport of supermoto, his new-found love, and I managed to con him into trying his hand at professional hillclimbing. I took him to Billings, Montana for the 2003 Great American Championship Hillclimb where 20,000 fans got to see him ride a 2500cc Harley-Davidson over the top. He's also tried car racing, serious trail riding with eight-time national enduro champion Dick Burleson, and has been working on more videos for his production company, Clutch Films. If anything, McGrath has one of the most interesting lives of anyone I know, and I certainly had a lot of fun writing about it and remembering things about the Jeremy I'd almost forgotten. I hope you enjoy!

—Ken Faught
January 2004

Chapter One

The BMX Years

Life as a Peddler

Jeremy was born in San Francisco. His dad, Jack McGrath, was into the illegal drag racing scene and was fascinated with speed and power. He loved his high-performance cars and trained as an auto mechanic at a local shop It was during this time that he met Ann, who later became his better half.

Jack also spent a lot of time riding street bikes and taught Jeremy's mom to ride. Jack had a Yamaha 360 MX dirt bike that he loved to ride in the hills on the outskirts of town. Jeremy's first motorcycling experience was riding double with his dad on that Yamaha 360 MX in Hollister, a small central California town that was the site of the infamous 1947 Hollister motorcycle riots that inspired the movie *The Wild Ones*. Jeremy was so small his feet couldn't touch the ground The pair would ride at a moderate pace with mom following behind on her Yamaha IT175.

Trophies, trophies, and more trophies—racing and winning have gone hand-in-hand anytime Jeremy has piloted something with wheels. Even at age 16, the family fireplace was covered. **Ann McGrath collection**

Jeremy's parents have been by his side throughout his entire career. Jack and Ann McGrath, shown here in 1974, provided everything MC needed for superstardom. **Ann McGrath collection**

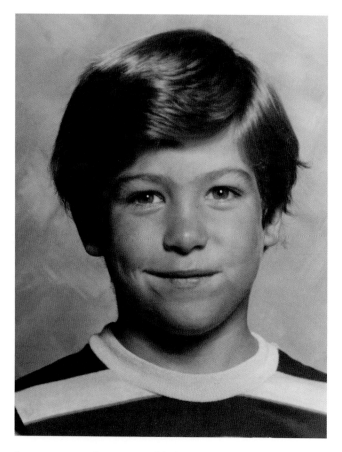

Supercross was only two years old when Jeremy's first grade photo was taken in 1976. **Ann McGrath collection**

After Jack finished learning the fine art of auto repair, the family left San Francisco for Southern California. They bought a house in Sun City on three acres and opened Jack & Ann McGrath's Auto Shop down the road.

One day, on Jack's way home from work, he saw a pair of mini-bike handlebars sticking out of the ground of someone's property. Jack stopped the car and discovered a complete bike buried in the ground. Jack talked to the owner of the land and asked if he could buy the rusting relic. The bike was really old and hadn't been started in years, but Jack bought it anyway. In his spare time, he started fixing it up and gave the orange machine to little Jeremy on his sixth birthday.

Jeremy learned to ride the Briggs & Stratton-powered machine in the parking lot of his parents' shop. He loved the machine, but the confines of the shop quickly made it monotonous. After a while, Jeremy parked his mini-bike and took up BMX. Even back then, the sport was really popular with all the neighborhood kids, and they rode every day after school.

By 1979, Jeremy was obsessed with bicycles. Then a kid named Jeff Castle, who lived in the neighborhood, got a new 1980 Yamaha YZ80. The state-of-the-art machine was radically different than Jeremy's lawnmower-engine-powered mini-bike. Jeremy told his dad about the new bike and managed to con him into buying him an updated motorcycle. Jack and Ann ended up buying him a used 1979 Suzuki RM80 that was functional and competitive.

Jack taught Jeremy about the transmission and how to use the clutch and five gears. Jeremy's BMX experience allowed him to adapt to the RM quickly. But since Jeremy didn't have a lot of kids to ride on his motorcycle with, he returned to BMX and his trusty human-powered Mongoose.

More time passed, and in 1981, Jeremy talked his parents into letting him race BMX for the first time. He entered the ten-year-old Beginner class and won. From that day on, he was addicted to the sport and began to develop his flashy style. Even at this young age, Jeremy loved to show off and Jack nicknamed him "Showtime."

"We were your normal kids back when we raced together," says Brian Lopes, now a two-time World Champion. "We were friends, but also competitors

Stick-and-ball sports were a part of Jeremy's life before he graduated to extreme sports. **Ann McGrath collection**

This may be the world's most expensive McGrath trading card. McGrath, 10, loved the San Diego Chargers and his favorite player, Dan Fouts. **Ann McGrath collection**

on and off the track. Our parents would hang out together at the races and we all had a good time. We've stayed friends over the years, and I think that's really cool. When we were racing, he was really good, but I still had him covered. I got the better end of him, but he was still really fast.

"Jeremy still loves to ride bicycles; in fact, we competed together in a No Fear team race a few years ago. It was when he was really into training, and he was really strong—I mean he was incredibly fit. He's got awesome drive, and he's just one of the most-talented overall athletes I've ever known."

Soon, Jeremy upgraded to a lighter weight Hutch bicycle. It didn't take long for him to advance through the ranks, and by the time he was 11, Jeremy was riding in the Expert class against other kids his age. Jeremy raced nearly a dozen times a week throughout Southern California at tracks like Coal Canyon BMX, Orange County YMCA, Snipes BMX, Corona YMCA, and Lake Elsinore BMX. Jeremy raced until he was 13 and talented enough to qualify for out-of-state Nationals. That year, Jeremy won the National Bicycle League Gold Cup and the California State Championship, even beating bicycle legend Brian Lopes. However, by the end of the 1984 season, Jeremy was tired of the hectic schedule and looking for a new challenge in the sporting world.

Jeremy, 11, had limited success in BMX, but it gave him a taste of competition. **Ann McGrath collection**

On November 19, 1985—Jeremy's birthday—his parents had a really big surprise. They took him outside and handed him a brand new 1986 Yamaha YZ80. Jeremy was shocked.

He played around with his new toy for a while before one of his BMX friends, Ray Hensley, talked him into racing motocross. In June, the McGraths headed to Perris Raceway, a track less than twenty minutes from their house. Jeremy entered the 80cc Beginner class and won the first moto, even beating some of the Novice riders that started a few seconds ahead of him on another row. In the second moto, the adrenaline must have been too much because Jeremy accidentally took off with the Novices. He finished third against the pack of faster riders and even beat Hensley. Jeremy wasn't awarded any points for the second moto, but he didn't care. He realized that he had found a new sport where he was competitive.

Jeremy (without helmet) loved two-wheeled racing, as shown in this 1982 photo. **Ann McGrath collection**

Jeremy McGrath's first bike rests in the showroom of Vintage Iron in Yorba Linda, California.
Ken Faught/Dirt Rider

At age 13, a young McGrath was already working on his style. **Ann McGrath collection**

Chapter Two

Life as an Amateur

Trial by Fire

After finding success at his first race, Jeremy became obsessed with motocross. The family owned a tractor, and they used it to make a jump-filled course on their 3-acre parcel of land. Jeremy's riding improved. He expanded his racing activities to become a regular at local tracks like De Anza and Glen Helen before looking for other challenges.

The McGrath's home off I-215 was near the epicenter of motocross. All the major manufacturers were less than two hours away, and most of the top racers in the world grew up, lived, or stayed in the region at some point in their careers. Motocross seemed to be everywhere, and within a two-hour drive there were more than a

As a teenager, McGrath spent several years on the amateur circuit at places like the NMA World Mini Grand Prix in Las Vegas. His first real bike deal came when Team Green offered him a contract to ride Kawasakis. **Ken Faught**

Even as an amateur in 1987, Jeremy drew a lot of attention at races like NMA's crown jewel in Ponca City, Oklahoma.
Ann McGrath collection

half-dozen race tracks, including Carlsbad and Barona Oaks. Many important regional race series and other big amateur events were in held in the area, too. It was at an event at Anaheim Stadium that I met Jeremy and his dad for the first time.

During Sunday's amateur program, I went to the Big A to watch a few of my friends race. At one point, a bunch of them were talking to some people I didn't know. I joined the group and set my Del Taco cup on the tailgate of a truck. Less than a minute later, a big biker-looking guy grabbed my Coke and took a swig. He sucked about half of it down before he realized that it wasn't his. The stranger looked at me and asked "Is this yours?" I nodded. Whether out of embarrassment or something else, he apologized, introduced himself as Jack McGrath, and invited me to their house to ride. I was 16 at the time and had just received my driver's license. I was working after school at a Yamaha dealership in Garden Grove called Orange County Cycle, and I managed to get him discounts on parts.

"Jeremy was one of the most popular amateurs in our area and he attracted a lot of attention everywhere he raced," says Daven Melendez, parts manager of the now defunct Orange County Cycle. "We helped him out as much as we could, even though he lived 60 miles from our shop. At that point of his career he was looking for anything he could get. I think we gave him 20 percent off on parts and accessories."

Practicing at home gave Jeremy an edge. He quickly graduated to the 125cc class and started riding with faster riders in the area. He raced in many events, from the Yamaha Classic MX Series to the Golden State Nationals. He knew the sport was expensive, but he also knew he had the ability to decrease the financial impact on his family by going faster and getting sponsors. About the same time, Yamaha introduced the YZ Bucks contingency program that offered riders a coupon good for parts and services at dealerships when they finished well in selected local events. While Yamaha spent a lot of money on contingency to promote its brand, the rest of the industry remained fairly conservative.

In 1986, Jeremy began to attract a lot of attention on the local level, but he went mostly ignored by major sponsors and factories. He combined his contingency with discounts at Orange County Cycle and Sunwest Sports, a Yamaha dealer in Corona, and managed to earn enough bonus bucks to buy a brand new 1987 Yamaha YZ80. Later that year, he earned enough to purchase a 1987 Yamaha YZ125.

Jeremy bypassed the Beginner class and went straight to 125cc Novice where he was fast enough to earn a title at the AMA Youth Amateur Nationals in Tennessee.

However, money lured Jeremy back to 80cc minis for one more race. A special event was held at Barona Oaks in San Diego on a hybrid supercross course. Jeremy rode 80cc

McGrath's home track in San Diego was Barona Oaks and it's where he was most feared in 1987. **Ann McGrath collection**

and 125cc bikes and managed to win three Honda Spree scooters for his impressive efforts. After that, he graduated to the Intermediate class and raced on big bikes permanently.

Little did he know, this era also produced his biggest rival—a kid named Jeff Emig. Jeremy raced against Emig all over the country, from the National Motosport Association (NMA) World Mini Grand Prix, to the Continental Motosport Club (CMC) Golden State Nationals, and back at Loretta Lynn's Dude Ranch in Tennessee. Jeremy was now racing full-time and devoting his life to motocross. Never interested in stick-and-ball sports, McGrath focused all of his efforts on the two-wheel world. He dreamed of someday being a factory rider for Team Honda and maybe winning a supercross or two.

"Jeremy and I had a lot of killer battles over the years," Emig says. "No matter if it was a local race or an amateur national, Jeremy and I gave it everything we had. Neither one of us like to lose, especially to the other guy. He's always had a lot of talent, and I knew I could trust him. Jeremy was a clean rider, and that made him a fun guy to race against."

Then came the weekend Jeremy names as "a big turning point in my career." It was a one-off race at Mammoth Lakes, California. He borrowed Ryan Carlisle's KX500 in order to ride three classes (125, 250, and Open). Unfortunately, Ryan's bike blew up, so Jeremy borrowed my Yamaha Pro Circuit-built YZ490. That weekend, Jeremy won seven of nine motos, and even beat Ryan Hughes, another kid from Southern California who was considered the top amateur in the region at the time. Hughes was a Team Green rider and got a half dozen bikes a year courtesy of Kawasaki. Jeremy had always been envious of Ryan's factory assistance and knew that winning Mammoth would prove a point—Jeremy McGrath should be taken seriously.

At the end of the 1988 season, McGrath made one of the biggest choices of his career. He decided to skip the usual path for talented riders and go straight to pro. Basically, Jeremy decided to stop racing the amateur circuit—the equivalent of college sports in the world of football, basketball, and baseball—and chase after money instead of trophies.

"I couldn't afford to race amateur full-time," says McGrath. "The only way I could pay for all my expenses was to move up. It was either make it or break it, and I knew I had to perform."

McGrath did get a Team Green ride and even raced in the now defunct Mickey Thompson Off-Road Championship Grand Prix series in a class called Ultracross. The national series featured off-road truck, buggy, and ATV racing, and motorcycles ran the course backwards on a man-made track inside stadiums like Anaheim, Houston, and Las Vegas. It wasn't exactly supercross, but Jeremy won some races, got some attention, and got a taste of racing in front of big crowds. He was also named "Man of the Year" by the Mickey Thompson series in 1989. Then, in 1989, Jeremy decided to make another move that would forever change his life. He headed toward Disneyland and signed up to race 125s at the Anaheim Supercross.

Jeremy won Loretta Lynn's 1987 125 Junior Class Championship in Tennessee aboard Yamahas his family bought. **Ann McGrath collection**

Tracy (junior high) poses with older brother Jeremy (high school). **Ann McGrath collection**

17

Chapter Three

Turning Pro

Life as a 125cc Supercross Specialist

In 1989, Jeremy made the decision to enter the sanitized world of stadium racing. He loaded up his pickup truck and headed to the Big A in Anaheim for a shot at 125cc Supercross stardom. He took his Pro Circuit-built production bike to a fourth place finish, which was impressive considering the other guys rode $35,000–50,000 works bikes and had more experience. Two weeks later, McGrath headed north to Washington State and managed to finish second behind Kawasaki's Jeff Matiasevich, marking the first podium finish of his young career.

Jeremy McGrath (No. 125) was part of Pro Circuit's first-ever factory Honda-supported race team along side of Steve Lamson (No. 29). This was the first time a company fitted all of its riders in identical clothing since Team Tamm disbanded in the mid-1980s. Also notice the glowing numbers, a gimmick that only lasted one season. **Ken Faught**

It took Jeremy McGrath several years to fully adapt to the outdoor national tracks like Hangtown in Northern California. Even though he already had a supercross championship under his belt at the time of this 1993 race, he wasn't a serious threat for the small-bore outdoor title. **Ken Faught/Dirt Rider**

McGrath honed his big-air skills on 125s and was one of the most confident racers to ever hit the track. **Fran Kuhn/Dirt Rider**

"I even surprised myself that first year," says McGrath. "I felt like I would be competitive, but it's always easier watching from the stands or on TV."

Shortly thereafter, his mom opened up a checking account with $500 and told Jeremy that he was old enough to manage his own money. The family continued to pay Jeremy's race expenses, with winnings going into Jeremy's checking account. Young Jeremy learned that racing could make him a profit, a lesson that served him well as his career advanced.

Jeremy landed a ride with Team Green in 1990. Jeremy had wanted to ride for the Kawasaki support program since he was an Intermediate, and now he had the ability to advance his career. Team Green's Mark Johnson gave Jeremy three bikes, a $500 allowance on parts purchased at cost, and access to team mechanics that would prep his race bikes.

During this one-year stint on Kawasaki, McGrath met Skip Norfolk, who spun wrenches for the amateur kids. McGrath had just finished high school and the two learned the fine art of testing at Jeremy's backyard practice track. Later, Skip even rented a house on the property, allowing the pair more time to perfect their skills.

Although Jeremy's contract was for amateur racing, he was able to race the AMA 125cc Western Region Supercross Series, which was a farm league for the 250cc class. "Showtime" raced all but one event of the eight-race series and finished second overall to Ty Davis, who later transitioned into cross-country racing. McGrath's finish proved that he was a legitimate title threat.

"I knew Jeremy was really talented, but never knew he would turn out to be the greatest supercross rider of all-time," Davis says. "He seemed to come out of nowhere and was incredibly good on technical tracks. He had a unique style that he refined over the years, and his aggressive approach changed the way everyone rode in the future. He's a champion's champion, and I'm proud to say that I was able to beat him for a No. 1 plate—that's one of the things I'm most proud of in my career."

McGrath's time with Kawasaki was good for his career. He attracted the attention he deserved

and got a very unexpected phone call one hot summer afternoon. Jeremy was in Tennessee for the Youth Amateur National Championship when former motocross/supercross great Rick Johnson gave him a ring. At first, Jeremy thought someone was playing a prank, but RJ asked Jeremy to ride for Honda and the pair soon struck a deal.

At the time of McGrath's Honda deal, he believed that it was a full factory deal for 1991–1992, but his contract was reassigned to Team Pro Circuit. **Fran Kuhn/Dirt Rider**

Originally, the program was supposed to be an in-house factory Honda ride alongside the 250 and 500cc riders Jean-Michel Bayle and Jeff Stanton. This was before 500s, known as Open class bikes, were forced into extinction because of AMA rule changes and dated technology. Shortly thereafter, the 125cc program was turned over to Mitch Payton at Pro Circuit. Honda and Pro Circuit formed a partnership whereby the team would hire four riders to compete on 125s. This was the start of factory-level support in this relatively new class (the 125 series started in 1985), but it wasn't welcome news for McGrath. Jeremy's entire family felt blindsided by the changes, but it was a serious shot at racing dirt bikes for a living.

Jeremy signed with Team Pro Circuit/Peak Honda for $35,000 a year and convinced Payton to hire Norfolk as his mechanic. Jeremy and teammates Brian Swink, Steve Lamson, and Jeromy Buehl tested at Honda's top-secret test track in Simi Valley, dubbed Hondaland. Jeremy and Skip started to understand Honda's corporate philosophy of winning at all costs and finding solutions instead of dwelling on problems.

Jeremy now had real works parts and one of the fastest bikes on the track, if not the fastest. He won

"I learned a lot from Jeremy. When we were teammates at Honda, he taught me a lot, and that gave me a lot of confidence. It's that confidence that allowed me to elevate my career, and he pushed me just as hard as I pushed myself."

—Steve Lamson, two-time AMA 125cc National Champion and former McGrath Honda and Chaparral teammate

The consummate play rider, Jeremy tried to do things other riders thought were impossible. If there were ever a motocross version of the H-O-R-S-E basketball game, MC would win hands down. **Ken Faught/ Dirt Rider**

A young MC interviewed during the 1991 Paris Supercross. **Ken Faught/Dirt Rider**

the series that season, bumping his salary to $55,000, and then he successfully defended the title in 1992. Even more impressive was the fact that he won his first title despite breaking his leg and separating his shoulder during the concurrent outdoor series. McGrath rode the supercross series finale in San Jose while injured. He needed to finish tenth or better to win the series if rival Jeff Emig won the race. In the end, Yamaha's Emig did win the race and Jeremy finished ninth and won his first No. 1 plate.

Jeremy did plenty of winning in the abbreviated series. He won 13 races in 125cc supercross, making him the all-time leader for victories in that category. For reference, Ricky Carmichael, Ernesto Fonseca, Damon Huffman, Brian Swink, and Kevin Windham are all tied for second with 12 wins each.

It was also during this time period that Jeremy landed his first major cover photo. I was working at *Cycle News* at the time as an associate editor. Jeremy's parents called me at work and asked what it would take to get him on the front page. The editor at the time was Jack Mangus, a hard-working 50-something guy who loved dirt track racing and the Cardinals baseball team. On a good day, he would do almost anything for you. If he was in a bad mood, you had better stay clear.

I told Jack McGrath to let me go through the photos from that weekend's race and to call me back in 15 minutes. I looked at my six black-and-white proof sheets and knew I had enough good shots to make something work. So when Jack called me back, I had him call Mangus to ask about putting Jeremy on the cover. I don't know if he made the call as Jeremy's dad or whether he played anonymous, but it worked.

A few minutes later, Mangus walked the 35 feet to my desk and asked, "Who won this week's 125 class?" He said he was thinking about putting "the winner" on the cover and pretended it was his idea. I knew he already had the answer, but I told him anyway. I pulled the proof sheets and he made the selection—a back shot of Jeremy heading into a turn. Five years later, after I left *Cycle News* for *Dirt Rider*, I told Mangus how we played him that day.

Jeremy always favored himself as a supercross rider. He loved jumps, technical obstacles, and had a way of connecting obstacles in a manner reserved for 250cc factory riders. He was also the master of the pivot turn and could dive in and out of the banked corners better than anyone else.

McGrath won his first supercross at Las Vegas in 1989. **Ann McGrath collection**

During his three-year stint riding 125s outdoors (including 1993 when he rode the small-bore class outside while riding 250cc supercross), the young phenom was held to two wins. At the beginning of the 2004 series, he ranked 31st on the All-time 125 National win list. This was the only class where he never won a series championship.

"I really didn't care much for the outdoors at first," says Jeremy. "To me, supercross was always the coolest form of motorcycle racing. It's what everyone talked about, and if you asked the riders which championship they would want to win, everyone in the world, including grand prix guys in Europe, would say supercross. The stadium held more fans, the atmosphere was more intense, and spectating was more enjoyable. It also got more television and press coverage. And for me, a lot of my friends would go and watch supercross long before they would consider going to a National. It was, and still is, the most important title in our sport."

"I know it really frustrated Jeremy not to do well outdoors," says Payton. "I know he played it off like he didn't care, but I know it bothered him deep inside. We would talk about it all the time, and he just couldn't figure it out at first."

After Jeremy won his first supercross title in 1993, he headed overseas for the Motocross des Nations in Austria. During that era, Jeremy and his dad Jack were almost inseparable. **Ann McGrath collection**

Three years, three consecutive supercross championships…Jeremy's mom, Ann, has been the backbone of the family and handed a lot of Jeremy's personal and business affairs. **Ann McGrath collection**

Skip Norfolk was McGrath's mechanic during the glory days. Arguably, this was the most successful pairing in all of motocross racing.
Ann McGrath collection

"I always loved working with Jeremy. He was one of the most gifted riders that I've ever seen, and he expected as much from us as we expected from him. He was an innovator, and he loved to do things on a motorcycle that others couldn't. He was really good for our sport and made it exciting. I'm not sure there will ever be another rider who does so much good for supercross or our sport."

—Mitch Payton, Pro Circuit Racing

Jeremy and his sister, Tracy, attended Skip's wedding in SoCal.
Ann McGrath collection

Skip was nervous during his wedding, but Jeremy helped calm his
nerves. **Ann McGrath collection**

McGrath spent a lot of his time watching other riders in the 250cc class, guys like Damon Bradshaw, Guy Cooper, and Honda teammates Jean-Michel Bayle and Jeff Stanton. Jeremy was fortunate enough to have two of the world's most talented riders on his team and managed to pick up a few tips from these dedicated champions.

"Honda's whole program is based on winning," says McGrath. "You either had to perform, or you were off the team. I knew I only had one shot, maybe two, and then I was gone. Honda was by far the most dominant team on the track. They had a reputation of building champions, and you didn't have the same odds on the track with any other team. In fact, one year Honda came out with shirts that said 'No Wing, No Prayer.'"

Team Honda, with its distinctive white wing on the radiator shroud, was the team of teams during this era. It was no surprise when Honda's Dave Arnold, the team manager at the time, called Jeremy for a 250 ride. It was then that Jeremy McGrath had what was unquestionably the best technology and bikes in the world, and he was about to show the veterans what he could do with it.

McGrath won all but one supercross in 1996 and claimed his record-setting fourth championship. **Ann McGrath collection**

International races paid Jeremy well during the off-season. The relaxed pace, in places like Milan, Italy, was a nice change of pace compared to United States competition. **Ann McGrath collection**

Chapter Four

Instant Success

MC Finds a Home in the 250cc Class

Riding the 250cc class was nothing new for Jeremy. He spent a lot of his amateur career on bigger

bikes, and they actually suited his aggressive style better than 125s. The challenge in supercross is

that obstacles are spaced much closer together than they are in outdoor motocross. This means a

miscue is more harmful since riders generally try to connect obstacles in stadium racing and don't have time to

recover before another hazard is upon them.

Jeremy's flashy riding style made him a crowd favorite all over the world. This is one of the first-ever Supermans, debuted in Paris, France, in 1996. **Ken Faught/Dirt Rider**

"I had to use the 125 class as a stepping stone to the 250 class," says McGrath. "None of the factories will hire you directly on to the 250 team without having 125 experience first. I really didn't mind it that much because I learned a lot during that time, and then I was able to do well from the minute I hopped on a 250."

McGrath's 250 supercross debut came in Daytona Beach, Florida, on March 7, 1992 while he was still contracted to ride 125s. He was on a confidence high after dominating the 125cc Western Region SX series for a year and a half.

"I wanted to test myself and see where I stood against all the other riders," says McGrath. "It's always easy to look at lap times, but they don't tell the whole story when you are on different size bikes. I also wanted to try something new and I wanted a bigger challenge. I was concerned that if I didn't race against faster guys, that I wouldn't be hungry enough to push myself further on a weekly basis."

The track at Daytona is unlike any other in the AMA Supercross Series. It's longer, creates higher speeds, and is mostly sand. It's a combination outdoor National track and supercross-style

"One of the best photo sessions of all time was at the Castillo Ranch in 1995," says McGrath. He and teammate Steve Lamson were there to film the first installment of the Terrafirma video series by Fox Racing. **Ken Faught/Dirt Rider**

The blue and gold No. 1 plate used to be reserved for the AMA Grand National Motocross Champ, but they used the color combo during the 1995 Paris Supercross. **Ken Faught/Dirt Rider**

course. It's also rough—really rough—which is a stark contrast to the perfectly prepared courses inside the domes of Indy and Dallas. McGrath finished 20th overall in a field of 30. The larger track actually allows ten more riders to start than in a normal supercross.

It's interesting to look back at who was in the race. It's not surprising that Jeff Stanton beat Damon Bradshaw and Jean-Michele Bayle, but the other players in the crowd are notable. Jeff Emig, McGrath's future rival finished eighth; Larry Brooks, MC's future team manager was 13th; current Grand National Cross Country (GNCC) star Fred Andrews was 21st; and the greatest Grand Prix rider of all, Stefan Everts, was 28th during a race appearance in the United States.

A week later, Jeremy tried it again at Charlotte, North Carolina. This time he finished tenth as Bayle edged out Stanton and Larry Ward. A week after that, McGrath finished sixth and continued his climb to the top. As if that wasn't impressive enough, he broke into the top five when the series stopped in Tampa.

On that Saturday evening, Jeremy actually led Jeff Stanton and Jean-Michel Bayle for a few laps during his heat race. Two hours later, he finished fourth in

It took McGrath several years to figure out how to be competitive in the outdoor series. **Ken Faught/Dirt Rider**

McGrath sealed his first supercross championship at the Pasadena Rose Bowl in 1993 and then celebrated with friends afterward at Chili's Bar & Grill. **Ken Faught/Dirt Rider**

the main event that silenced those who questioned his speed and conditioning. Main events in the 250cc class are 20 laps compared to 15 laps in the 125cc class. To be a contender, Jeremy had to push himself five minutes longer and be virtually mistake-free the entire time.

Two weeks later, McGrath finished eighth and sixth, respectively, during the Pontiac double-header. That was the last opportunity for him to ride 250s before the 125cc Western Region SX series resumed.

At the end of the 1992 season, Jean-Michel Bayle shocked the motocross community and announced that he was headed to Europe to try his hand at road racing. Bayle figured his near-effortless style would put him at the top of the pack someday, though it didn't turn out that way. Bayle's departure left a void at Team Honda and McGrath was hired to fill the vacancy.

"I would have been hired no matter what," says Jeremy. "But when JMB left, I think they realized they needed me more now than ever. It's a good thing to feel wanted, especially when it's Honda that needs your services."

In September 1992, Jeremy said goodbye to Team Pro Circuit/Peak Honda and finally climbed into a factory box van. His No. 15 CR250 was a factory bike from the graphics all the way down to the works Dunlop tires. It was loaded with all sorts of titanium, magnesium, and other featherweight fasteners not available to the public.

"You can't believe the difference between a production bike and a works bike back in that era," says Jeremy. "The bike was just incredible. The motor was fast, and the suspension sucked up almost everything. It just gives you a lot of confidence and allows you to try things you normally wouldn't attempt."

In February 1995, McGrath was already well on his way to winning his third-consecutive title for Honda. **Ken Faught/Dirt Rider**

Jeremy "Showtime" McGrath went into the 1993 season hell-bent on winning races and trying to dethrone the champ, Jeff Stanton. But Stanton was still in his prime, and so was Kawasaki's Mike Kiedrowski. Although many felt Kiedrowski was an outdoor specialist, he came into his own during the early 1990s and wanted a supercross title to round out his portfolio. Though he does own 125, 250, and 500cc AMA National Championships, Kiedrowski never did win the 250cc AMA Supercross title.

The 1993 season started off well for McGrath. He traveled 2300 miles to Orlando from his new home in Murrieta, California, and managed to finish fourth aboard his first-ever full-on works Honda 250. A week later, the series headed to Houston and McGrath placed fifth. Jeremy was doing well by rookie standards, but he wasn't used to losing. He knew he could run with Stanton during Honda testing and felt that he should be at the front of the field battling with his superstar teammate.

Round three of the series headed to the West Coast to a track Jeremy called home. It was Anaheim Stadium, and all of McGrath's friends and family were in attendance. Jeremy got off to a good start and managed to pass Stanton for the lead. Eventually, McGrath stretched out his lead enough to score the first win of his career. January 23, 1993, will always be remembered as the day Jeremy McGrath began what would become the winningest career of any supercross rider in history.

While Jeremy was spraying champagne, he was unaware of the drama unfolding with his dad. After

Jeremy crossed the finish line, Jack McGrath jumped over the railing and onto the track to join the celebration. That's when the 260-pound McGrath was confronted by several security officers. Jack tried to push the guards away, but was handcuffed and escorted to a holding room. He was detained for a half hour before they finally figured out who he was and let him go without filing charges.

"I was pretty upset that night after he beat me," Stanton says. "I knew Jeremy was fast, but up until that point he didn't have the confidence to win. Usually, once you figure out how to win, you're able to do it again and again. He was really young at the time, and I think it surprised a lot of people how fast he adapted to 250s."

Round four of the series headed to Seattle, Washington, where Jeremy hole shot and raced away from the field. Then he won at San Diego and Tampa, where he'd made his 250 debut just one year earlier.

Jeremy had a shot at making history as the AMA tour headed to Atlanta. Win this race and he would be the only rider in history to win five supercross main events back-to-back.

He was already tied with Bob Hannah, Rick Johnson, and Damon Bradshaw for winning four straight. Unfortunately, Jeremy finished fourth, but that was enough to give him something even more important—the series points lead.

The next stop was Daytona Beach, Florida, on the infield of the famous NASCAR stadium. This is a rough sand track that resembles something found on the AMA National Championship Series, not supercross. McGrath finished second, but knew it wouldn't be long before he returned to his winning ways.

During the entire season, he continued to work on his style. He created the brake-tap technique, where he could adjust the attitude of the bike in mid-flight to stay lower than the other riders on 70-foot triple jumps. He also introduced the Nac-Nac, one of the many moves McGrath created that helped spawn the freestyle revolution. Motocross and supercross were starting to gain more popularity in the United States, and Jeremy McGrath was the draw. He quickly learned how to entertain sold-out crowds and was certainly living up to his Showtime nickname.

McGrath won Dallas and Charlotte, and one of two nights during the Pontiac doubleheader in Michigan. Then he won Indianapolis and wrapped up the title two races early with a win in Pasadena. After the race, about two dozen of us went to a Chili's restaurant to celebrate, courtesy of Honda. It was unreal to see a rookie win the 250cc title and do it in such convincing style.

He also won San Jose, which tied him once again with most consecutive AMA wins. He had another

When MCI's 1-800-COLLECT division began sponsoring Team Honda, they asked MC to film a commercial in the pits of Las Vegas the day of the supercross. **Ken Faught/Dirt Rider**

shot to extend his win-streak in Las Vegas, but could only manage ninth behind former champ Jeff Stanton in his last career win.

"I still can't get over that season," says McGrath. "Everything just fell into place. Skip [Norfolk] and I were kind of caught off guard, but we didn't allow anything to affect us. We just wanted to win races and championships. I focused everything on supercross and on 250s. I still rode the 125 class outdoors, but I really didn't enjoy it that much. I tried like I always do, but 250 supercross meant everything to me. That's where you earn respect, and I wanted to repeat over and over again."

McGrath returned to Orlando, Florida, in 1994 with a No. 1 plate on his bike. Everyone knew he was in a league of his own and he was officially the guy to beat. He was young, hungry, and innovative. He was also healthy and planned on riding 250s full-time in both series. This meant he could spend more time on the works Honda CR250 and have more intimate knowledge of its capabilities and behavior.

"It's a lot harder to switch bikes back and forth than people think," says McGrath. "A 125 and 250 handle different; the power isn't close to being the same, and you have to ride them with a different style. A 125 you have to use more momentum, but 250s you can make up more creative lines, which allows you to make more aggressive passes."

But passing wasn't a skill McGrath really needed. He quickly earned a reputation as a "hole shot artist." In laymen's terms, he could launch out of the starting gate faster than anyone else

McGrath won 8 of 12 Nationals in 1996, but finished the season second overall because of an injury that held him to sixth at Millville and 15th at Washougal.
Dirt Rider

Above and opposite: Even the champ makes mistakes on occasion. During the filming of Fox Racing's Terrafirma video, McGrath over-jumped this double and couldn't bring the back end around in time to make a safe landing. **Ken Faught/Dirt Rider**

and win the critical drag race to the first turn, and he could do it on a regular basis. In fact, early critics wondered if Jeremy could win without getting a hole shot. As always, McGrath soon proved that he could do just about anything, even winning after starting 16th!

McGrath won Orlando, then Houston, Anaheim, and San Diego. For the third time in his career, he was tied with Hannah, Johnson, and Bradshaw for consecutive wins, but wanted the record all to himself. He spanked them in Florida, got the record, and then won the following race in Atlanta. Jeremy was truly a special rider and was headed for his second consecutive title.

Next was Daytona, Jeremy's least favorite track. "I never went to Daytona thinking that I could win there early in my career," says McGrath. "It just wasn't my style. I didn't like the sand and didn't have much time to practice under those conditions." McGrath placed fourth but won the next race in Indianapolis.

During the following seven races, McGrath only won three times, but still captured the title.

Outdoors was a whole different story. Although McGrath preferred the 250cc class, he found the competition much harder than the AMA 125cc Nationals. Of the 12 races in the series, McGrath didn't win a single one. He managed to finish the series with third overall, but found Mike Kiedrowski and Mike LaRocco too fast on the high-speed courses.

The 1995 season proved to be another record-breaker for young Jeremy, especially after Jeff Stanton and Damon Bradshaw both retired. McGrath won the first five races (nine in all), and he didn't even race Las Vegas. A power failure knocked out electricity all over town, including Sam Boyd Stadium. The unplanned event forced promoters to postpone the event until they managed to rent portable light units. Many of the racers started talking about boycotting the 20-lap final, including McGrath, who felt the dimly lit course wouldn't be safe.

Fans didn't know it at the time, but McGrath and several other riders left the track expecting the other factory riders to follow suit. After all, the riders had agreed to boycott. But not all of them kept their word. In the end, Yamaha's Jeff Emig won, which gave him the first 250cc AMA Supercross win of his career, albeit a very controversial one. McGrath had already won his third consecutive SX title, which tied him with Bob Hannah (1977-1979) as the only rider to win it three times in a row. Jeremy also tied Hannah for second on the all-time supercross win list with a victory in Charlotte, and then two rounds later tied Rick Johnson for first. Jeremy scored that many wins in three seasons while it took RJ twice as long.

"I was really excited with the way things were going," says Jeremy. "My confidence was really up and I felt like I didn't have much to prove. I knew I was the best at supercross and knew I had to step things up outdoors. Honda really wanted to win the 250cc National Championship and strongly encouraged me to spend more time testing and practicing. Skip also knew it was important, and told me that if I could just win one race that I could probably have the confidence to win the championship."

The 1995 AMA 250cc National MX Championship started out at Gainesville, Florida, in the middle of an abandoned quarry. Although the track was extremely fast and rough, it had a bunch of supercross-style obstacles and blind jumps. Jeremy managed to win his first-ever 250cc National that day, which did change his outlook on the 12-race series. During that season he won eight races, including Budds Creek, Red Bud, Troy, and Unadilla. He also won the final three races of the year at Washougal, Binghamton, and Steel City, and finally earned his first No. 1 plate outdoors.

McGrath won his first outdoor title in 1995, and did so in the 250cc class. He spent much of his time battling with Jeff Emig, who he's chasing here at Hangtown. **Ken Faught/Dirt Rider**

Even the mud at Mt. Morris didn't affect Jeremy, who grew up racing on the hard-packed tracks of Southern California. Although he finished third during the third round of the series, he still left Pennsylvania with the series points lead. **Ken Faught/ Dirt Rider**

"I was so pumped that year," says Norfolk. "Things really came together for the whole team." In fact, Steve Lamson, McGrath's teammate, won the 125cc Championship that year in dominant fashion. The Honda Racing Dynasty was in full effect, and Jeremy was captain of the most powerful team of that era. He was so strong that no one questioned whether he would win or not in 1996; it was just a matter of by how many points he would beat second place. Jeremy perfected the gutsy move of skimming whoops, introduced BMX techniques into jumping, and was cornering faster than anyone in history. His bike was also the best, and every one of McGrath's competitors knew it.

He started off by winning the first five races of the season in dominant style. He stretched the streak to six, then seven, then eight. Soon, the entire motocross world was watching as the millionaire Honda superstar made history. People couldn't wait to find out whether he had recorded another win or whether the streak was finally over. In March he recorded win nine, followed by ten, 11, and 12. When round 13 drew near, many predicted the "unlucky number" would end the impressive run, but it didn't. The winning streak ended in St. Louis at the hands of Jeff Emig. The factory Kawasaki rider had long been Jeremy's arch rival, and it was only fitting that Jeffro would be the spoiler. Jeremy did win the season finale, giving him a record 14 wins in a single season, but it

Jeff Stanton spent a lot of time in 1993 chasing McGrath. Stanton routinely followed the young superstar in practice to study his lines and check out his technique. **Ken Faught/Dirt Rider**

didn't matter much to the now four-time champ. His season ended with an average finish of 1.066666th place.

"I really wanted to win every single race," says McGrath. "I never thought it was possible until I got to round ten. From that point on, I only cared about the win streak and the record. I knew I was making history, and it got our sport of a lot of attention. It was absolutely incredible and was almost perfect…almost being the key word."

"Jeremy was completely in a league of his own in 1996," Roger DeCoster says. "Jeremy was the hottest thing the sport had ever seen, and he was exactly what supercross needed. Luck didn't have much to do with anything—Jeremy was just that much better than his competition that year."

The outdoor series started off as planned for the new rider with the No. 1 plate. Jeremy won Gainesville, Hangtown, and Glen Helen. He had problems at Mt. Morris and finished third, but then won Budds Creek, Southwick, and Red Bud. Seven races into the series, he had scored victories in all but one event. He placed second at Unadilla, won Troy, and then headed to Minnesota where the unexpected happened. During practice, Jeremy attempted a jump that no one has tried again to this date. It was a single jump preceding a large tabletop, and Jeremy tried to clear the entire gap. He came up way short and slammed his neck on the crossbar. He also injured his foot, but surprisingly, came away with no broken bones.

"I still don't know why I tried it," says McGrath. "I guess I just felt unstoppable. I didn't even have to do it. It was just something I wanted to prove to everyone. I wanted them to see that I was in a league of my own in every aspect. I guess I wanted to do something that would blow their minds."

McGrath has always been the consummate showman. During the 1993 Glen Helen National, he entertained fans during practice over this small step-up double. **Ken Faught/Dirt Rider**

McGrath became the first motocross rider in history to make over $10 million dollars. He continues to make money today even though he's retired. **Ken Faught/Dirt Rider**

One of the things that made McGrath so great was his willingness to push the envelope. He often tried jumps that other people wouldn't consider, and that elevated the level of racing at the top. **Ken Faught/ Dirt Rider**

He still raced two days later, but was way off the pace. Riding in pain, Jeremy finished sixth and knew the championship was slipping away.

In Washington, Jeremy placed 15th at Washougal's famous hill-and-valley circuit, and things were looking ugly for the defending champ. When the series traveled to upstate New York, the old McGrath returned. Although he still wasn't totally healthy, he managed to suck up the pain and win the event. That set up one of the most dramatic series finales in AMA history.

Going into Steel City, Jeremy led Emig by a mere point. Whoever won the day would win the overall. Jeremy was still in a lot of pain and knew he couldn't dab his foot.

Jeremy hole shot the first moto and led for 20 minutes. Emig was behind him the whole time, hoping McGrath would

McGrath takes a look at the 1996 Motocross des Nations in Jerez, Spain. **Ken Faught/Dirt Rider**

Jeremy was one of the first riders to master the bump-seat technique for jumps. This is a method of compressing the rear suspension deeper into the travel on takeoff so it will "bounce" you over a much taller second jump. **Ken Faught/Dirt Rider**

make a mistake, but finally forced a move. Emig passed McGrath in a corner, and then flew to the checkered flag. Emig was now in the points lead and MC had to win the final moto to win the title.

Emig got the better start in moto two, but many witnesses claimed he cut over on McGrath with a dirty move.

"I rode in second for most of the race until Greg Albertyn passed me," says McGrath. "I was completely bummed and knew it was over unless Emig were to crash. He didn't, and I lost the title. Basically, I lost the title in Millville, and then sealed the deal at Washougal. I gave it my all, but I just couldn't come back after the crash. That's one of the few years I wish I could redo, well, at least half of it."

Emig was responsible for costing Jeremy his first No. 1 plate and now stopping the perfect supercross season. McGrath wanted to get him back, but his racing program soon changed dramatically.

During the previous few years, there had been a lot of changes at Team Honda. Roger DeCoster left to run Suzuki's race program, and team manager Dave Arnold left for a bicycle company, then returned to Honda, but in the research and development division. Wes McCoy was now a team manager, and the entire McGrath family did not like him. McCoy was heavily involved with Honda's ATV race program before the demise of three-wheelers in 1987. Wes was all Honda and all corporate and brought a lot of tension to the team. Wes took the fun out of racing and made it seem like work to the young riders.

Fresh after teaming up with Steve Lamson and Jeff Emig to win the Motocross des Nations in Jerez, Spain, Jeremy got a copy of his revised factory contract in late November 1996. McGrath says he had a verbal agreement on a two-year deal that would pay him about a million dollars a season, but now there were new restrictions—in Jeremy's words "12-pages worth." Although no one except Honda, Jeremy's family, and his lawyers have ever seen the actual document, McGrath says it basically dictated what he could do on and off the track. He says it wouldn't allow him to ride BMX, personal watercraft, wakeboard, or participate in any of the other thrill sports that were a huge part of his lifestyle. McGrath says he spent $8000 in lawyers' fees just to understand the complicated legalese. By the time the lawyers had explained the new contract to the McGrath family, it was mid-December 1996.

McGrath was beyond upset. He was pissed off and wanted to make Honda pay. He couldn't believe the control Honda was trying to get over his career. Things were going so well, and now his short- and long-term future was in question.

A week later, it was time to test Honda's all-new 1997 CR250. Honda had abandoned the traditional steel frame and went with an aluminum twin-spar design that many experts considered revolutionary at the time. In reality, the bike wasn't that good and Jeremy had difficulties riding the machine. I remember

Skip Norfolk was the ideal mechanic for McGrath. He kept Jeremy grounded and gave him nearly bulletproof equipment to race. **Ken Faught/Dirt Rider**

You won't find a dad at the races more proud than Jack McGrath. Along with Jeremy's mom, Ann, and sister Tracy, the family sacrificed a lot for Jeremy's success. **Ken Faught/Dirt Rider**

43

Troy Lee gave Jeremy this one-off helmet for the Anaheim supercross in 1996. The paint scheme featured $100 bills on each side, and soon, kids all over the world tried to duplicate the look using $1 bills. **Ken Faught/Dirt Rider**

Jeremy's mechanic accidentally brought his wife's passport to the airport in 1996 for a trip to Paris, France. That left MC and best friend Lawrence Lewis to figure out how to make the all-new aluminum-frame 1997 CR250R work. **Ken Faught/Dirt Rider**

Jeremy hated the aluminum frame on the 1997 CR250R and told his mom in a phone call after Bercy that he didn't think he could win on the bike. The new course of technology that Honda chose made it easier for McGrath to leave the Red Rider's program and look elsewhere for factory support. **Ken Faught/Dirt Rider**

going to the Paris Supercross with him in Bercy and listening to his frustrations. When Skip Norfolk showed up at the airport, he accidentally brought his wife's passport. The only thing Jeremy could do was call his best friend/roommate Lawrence "Lew" Lewis and ask him to spin wrenches for the weekend. Lew barely made the flight, but didn't have time to pack his bags. He stayed in Jeremy's room so the two could share clothes.

The Nac-Nac quickly became MC's signature move, and he usually threw one out during opening ceremonies and whenever he won a race.
Ken Faught/Dirt Rider

Jeremy's first 250cc National win came at Gainesville, Florida, in March 1995, and 11 races later he was crowned champ. **Ken Faught/Dirt Rider**

One of the things that made McGrath so fast was his ability to stay lower than other riders on 70-foot triple jumps. **Ken Faught/Dirt Rider**

Jeremy came to my room every night so he and his sister Tracy could call their parents. That Saturday night, I listened to McGrath tell his mom and dad that he couldn't win on the bike. He fell several times during the three-day weekend and couldn't blitz through the whoops in his usual fashion. Basically, he said the bike was unforgiving and "sucked." To make matters worse, he couldn't use his old chassis like he had throughout most of his career. With the exception of a short stint in 1995, Jeremy used a 1993 frame in 1993, 1994, and 1995. From the outside, people couldn't tell, but there was no way MC or Honda could camouflage the new heavy-duty aluminum chassis.

Things continued to deteriorate when Jeremy went to Japan and couldn't ride the bike there either. He fell time and time again and still had contractual woes weighing heavily on his mind.

Jeremy was the most sought-after commodity in two-wheel racing history. Every team wanted him and was willing to do just about anything to get him. In the end, Jeremy walked away from Team Honda, turning his back on them like they had done to him. It was, and still is, one of the most unlikely moves by any manufacturer in the history of the sport. The loss of McGrath officially ended Honda's racing dynasty and forced MC to change teams just three weeks before the season, which raised questions as to whether or not he could adapt to a new machine in time. Jeremy's long-time mechanic, Skip Norfolk, also decided to retire. Things were certainly changing, and changing fast.

In the pits of many overseas supercrosses, the riders are given a 10x10 spot for their bike and equipment. **Ken Faught/Dirt Rider**

The infamous Dallas supercross in 1995 was one of muddiest races of all-time. Conditions were so bad that riders put hand-made numbers on top of their helmets to help AMA officials score the race. **Ken Faught/Dirt Rider**

Jeremy celebrated his 1993 Charlotte supercross win with a no-hander that the North Carolina fans loved. **Ken Faught/Dirt Rider**

Right: Playriding is what helped spawn the freestyle movement that began taking off in the mid-1990s. Jeremy is one of the few riders who can whip a bike upside down and still recover. **Ken Faught/Dirt Rider**

Left: McGrath did about a dozen Nac-Nacs a few feet away from a tractor bucket where the photographer was standing on this day at the Castillo Ranch. This angle of the freestyle trick has rarely been seen. **Ken Faught/Dirt Rider**

MC always struggled at the high-speed supercross track at Daytona, but it didn't matter much in 1993. As a rookie, he was the rider to beat in the Camel supercross championship. **Mark Kariya/Dirt Rider**

McGrath celebrated a lot of wins in 1993. **Ken Faught/Dirt Rider**

The King of Supercross is the most marketable rider of all-time. The bikes he rides and the gear he wears always sell well for his sponsors. **Ken Faught/Dirt Rider**

McGrath preps his starting gate to make sure everything is functioning properly. **Ken Faught/Dirt Rider**

McGrath spent a lot of time testing, which is paramount for any racer to be successful. **Ken Faught/Dirt Rider**

McGrath does a big one-legged whip at Perris Raceway in Southern California. **Ken Faught/Dirt Rider**

Jeremy's best results came at outdoor tracks like Red Bud which feature big stadium-style jumps. **Ken Faught/Dirt Rider**

The early Nac-Nacs, such as this one at Anaheim Stadium in 1994, didn't have the incredible leg extension that McGrath was known for at the end of his career. **Donnie Bales**

McGrath debuted his blue and gold No. 1 plate in January 1994 at the Orlando supercross in Florida. **Ken Faught/Dirt Rider**

Testing, testing, and more testing—that has always been one of the fundamentals of Honda's racing effort. In 1993, McGrath spent a lot of time at Honda's private supercross track in Corona, California with Jeff Stanton and Steve Lamson. **Ken Faught/Dirt Rider**

The first 250cc National McGrath entered was at Gainesville, Florida, in 1994. He finished sixth overall and battled with guys like John Dowd (No. 16) that he normally wouldn't see during a supercross. **Mark Kariya/Dirt Rider**

McGrath whips it flat during a 1994 heat race win. Notice the stands are empty at this event in 1994.
Mark Kariya/ Dirt Rider

Chapter Five

Switching to Suzuki

McGrath Runs His Own Race Team

After leaving the ugly situation at Honda, the four-time AMA 250cc Supercross champ had his choice of teams. After all, he was the most dominant rider in the sport's history and was on top of his game.

As time ran out, Suzuki seemed to be McGrath's best option. He'd known team manager Roger DeCoster since his early Honda days, and he liked DeCoster's intense work ethic. DeCoster, himself a five-time World Champion, managed to turn Suzuki's race program around, and the works RM250 was viewed as a fairly competitive machine.

McGrath's struggles with the Suzuki seemed to be settling down at the 1997 Daytona supercross, where McGrath nailed the hole shot and then edged out Jeff Emig and Ezra Lusk to take the top podium spot. That win put him within 16 points of series leader Jeff Emig. **Ken Faught/Dirt Rider**

My father-in-law is Mel Harris, the head of American Suzuki. Basically, he's DeCoster's boss' boss, and is the key decision maker at the motorcycle giant. As talks turned into negotiations, I was getting a lot of information from both sides. Jack and Ann McGrath were asking me a lot of questions about Suzuki operations, policies, licensing, marketing, and just about everything one could imagine. Mel Harris was doing the same thing about the McGraths, and I had to watch what I said. I had everything to lose, nothing to gain, and no control over anything that happened.

It's hard for Mel and me to work in the same industry in our current positions. As the Editor-in-Chief of *Dirt Rider* magazine, I always have to watch how other companies view my relationship with Suzuki. I have to make sure there is no bias, especially when it comes to bike testing. Mel has to make sure that his people don't feel that I'm getting special treatment, and that isn't always easy. I always get the feeling from Suzuki personnel that they think Mel tells me everything before he tells them.

Throughout negotiations with the McGraths, Mel stayed true to form and wouldn't give me any new details. But Mel didn't fully understand my history with the McGraths, and soon he knew I had more details than he'd intended to share.

A racer leaving Team Honda was almost unimaginable, but McGrath left the company at the end of 1996 when he felt they were putting too many stipulations in his contract. **Ken Faught/Dirt Rider**

McGrath struggled at the beginning of the season with his new Suzuki. He only had a few days testing time before the season kicked off inside the Los Angeles Coliseum. **Ken Faught/Dirt Rider**

I was talking to Ann on the phone while driving down the 71 Expressway in Norco, California. She told me that Suzuki was offering Jeremy a $275,000 championship bonus—more than double what Jeremy got from Honda. A few days later, Mel and I were talking and I asked why they were offering so much. Stunned, he said, "Let's put it this way, we haven't paid out a lot of bonus money in the last ten years." It was sad, but true. Suzuki hadn't exactly been racking up championships in motocross or supercross. In fact, the last title came in 1990 at the hands of Guy Cooper in the AMA 125cc National Championship.

Few people knew of the negotiations with Suzuki. I had a huge scoop and knew it would help me sell magazines. I tried to get Mel to tell me that things were firm, but he kept saying that nothing was done until the ink on the contract was dry.

"I was actually a little concerned about the *Dirt Rider* cover," Harris says. "Although we thought we had a deal, we've been in similar situations before that didn't pan out. I actually told Ken [Faught, editor-in-chief] not to run it on the cover, but I guess he felt confident with the information he was given by the McGraths. He took a big chance, and it paid off for him."

I hired Tracy McGrath, Jeremy's sister, to shoot photos of a secret testing session at McGrath's house in December. Roger DeCoster, Hide Suzuki, and Ian Harrison took a works RM250 to Jeremy's house so he could ride the bike. Tracy and Ann came over a few days later to show me the photos. It was on this day, sitting in my living room, that Ann showed me the actual contract. It was the first time that I had ever seen a factory contract and all of its details. I was pumped, but it still hadn't been approved by Suzuki of Japan.

The January 1997 issue of *Dirt Rider* went to press with a cover that screamed, "Suzuki Steals McGrath: the inside story on why the champ abandoned Honda," and photos of Jeremy riding the bike inside. With the contract yet unapproved, it was a bit of a risk, but we beat everyone else with the news.

Two weeks later, Mel finally told me that Jeremy's Suzuki deal was done. Jeremy would ride factory bikes for his own team. He would run Suzuki of Troy graphics because they kicked in $200,000 directly to Jeremy, and the effort was run out of Suzuki's ultra-plush semi.

Team Kawasaki's Jeff Emig, a long-time rival of McGrath's, emerged as the new title favorite. **Ken Faught/Dirt Rider**

McGrath's Troy Lee Bell helmet. **Ken Faught/Dirt Rider**

Wyatt Seals, who also worked for Jeff Stanton and Ryan Hughes, spun the wrenches for McGrath at the start of the Suzuki deal. **Ken Faught/ Dirt Rider**

McGrath started experimenting with an eight-disc clutch pack before the Indianapolis event. Team Manager Roger DeCoster, himself a five-time World Champ, worked with MC and mechanic Wyatt Seals to solve the clutch-slipping problem. The fix came from Ron and Wayne Hinson who later turned their clutch innovations into a cottage industry and a company called Hinson Racing. **Ken Faught/Dirt Rider**

Unfortunately, Jeremy didn't have much time for testing. The supercross season kicked off at the Los Angeles Memorial Coliseum the first week of January, and that only left a few days to test. Every one of Jeremy's sponsors scrambled to pull off the deal, and it worked. He hired Wyatt Seals as his mechanic. Wyatt had worked for Ryan Hughes and Jeff Stanton and was well respected in the industry.

The sport of supercross changed forever with the first race of the 1997 season. Jeremy proved that he could get bikes and money to run his own team, something that was later emulated by Emig, Mike LaRocco, and a few others. It gave McGrath more control over his race program, but it also gave him more headaches. He also proved that he was the big draw at supercross. The Honda pits were all but empty, and there was now a huge line around the Suzuki semi. People waited as long as four hours to get Jeremy's autograph and catch a glimpse of his works RM250 hoisted onto the trailer's lift gate. Everything about Jeremy's program was different from Suzuki's other riders Greg Albertyn, Mike LaRocco, and Mickael Pichon. The official name of Jeremy's team was 1-800-COLLECT/Suzuki of Troy/No Fear. McGrath didn't have to abide by the same rules and had more freedom with setup, outside sponsors, and appearances.

All eyes were on Jeremy McGrath on January 11 as the main event began. This was the moment of truth; the one that would decide whether or not he made the right move. Jeremy shot out of the gate and had the hole shot going into the first turn. As McGrath leaned his bike over, Steve Lamson slammed him in the 90-degree turn. Lamson still rode for Honda and immediately accusations started to fly about a "bounty" on Jeremy's head.

The hit knocked Lamson down and left his bike stuck in Jeremy's rear wheel. By the time McGrath got going, he was in 19th place. He fell by himself two turns later, and that allowed Lamson to catch up. Lamson hit him again, and things went downhill fast.

"The first turn deal wasn't intentional," Lamson said during our 2003 interview. "My bike just hooked into his back wheel. He dragged me for a while, and then he stopped. That actually was an accident, and I could see why he was bummed because he did have the hole shot. Then, he fell two turns later all by him-self. We went up the pecistyle...we're half a lap be-hind, and he's yelling obscenities to me as we went through the top. And at the bottom there was a little step-up jump, and he made a crazy pass on me; I moved out of the way. I was pretty pissed at that time. So when I went over the triple, I didn't shut off, and then when we came to the next double into the bowl corner I just jumped to the inside of him and didn't stop. I was so fired up that I didn't care if I knocked his ass over or not. Plain and simple, I took him out."

Suzuki of Troy kicked in $250,000 for McGrath and his deal to race RM250s. Even though McGrath raced out of the factory semi in 1997, he still had the ability to select most of his own sponsors.
Ken Faught/Dirt Rider

This shot was taken in a makeshift studio under the Los Angeles Coliseum the day of the season opener. The graphics were literally finished the day before and hand-carried to the race.
Ken Faught/ Dirt Rider

Mud was never one of Jeremy's strong suits, but he was still able to hold his own when it got wet and slippery. **Dirt Rider**

Come the Washougal National in August, McGrath was already making plans for another ride. **Ken Faught/Dirt Rider**

At the end of the 20 laps, Jeremy finished a disappointing 15th and realized that he might have problems.

This was the first chance Jeremy had to measure himself and the RM250 against his competitors. Although he got the hole shot, an indication the bike was somewhat fast, there were other problems. Jeremy was accustomed to Honda torque and liked to ride his bike a gear high and slip the clutch a lot. The works RM250 couldn't handle the abuse, and the clutch would fade in a matter of minutes. Suzuki soon fabricated a quick adjuster on the perch, which now comes stock on most motocross bikes, but that was only a short-term fix.

Jeremy went to round two of the series, hoping to improve on the results. It too was at the Coliseum because it could hold over 100,000 spectators and held the first supercross event in 1972. This time Jeremy got third. It was good, but it was far from the dominant season he had in 1996 when he won 14 of 15 races. Jeremy began to doubt himself, his bike, and his decisions. He also wondered if he had to watch his back for another Honda attack.

Jeremy knew that Honda was so upset it was targeting anyone who helped MC. The company penalized Phil Alderton and his Ohio dealership by pulling all of its support. Back then, the team was called Honda of Troy, even though it was a multi-brand dealership. Jeremy's private team was sponsored by Suzuki of Troy, which Alderton also owned, so it was pretty obvious

McGrath felt his Suzuki lacked low-end and mid-range power, yet he still rode to second in the championship and won several main events. **Ken Faught/Dirt Rider**

In December 1996, Suzuki had a semi-secret testing session with McGrath at his parents' home in southern California. Jeremy's parents built a supercross track on their property, and this marked the first time MC rode a works RM250. **Tracy McGrath**

what Honda was doing. (The team is now called Yamaha of Troy, and is one of the most successful programs of the modern era.)

Jeremy went to Tempe and finished second; he finished in the same spot a week later in Seattle. Round five headed to Indianapolis, and the track was extremely tacky and full of traction. Again, clutch problems proved problematic and held McGrath to ninth. Suzuki hired Wayne Hinson of Hinson Racing to build an eight-disc clutch pack, hoping this would be a cure. The clutch pack had one extra set of plates, but took a while to perfect. Little did they know, this venture put Wayne Hinson and his son, Ron, into the successful business of building aftermarket clutches full-time. (Ironically, they've sponsored Team Honda for several years.)

McGrath was under a lot of pressure during this testing session. He was trading in his works Hondas for something totally different, and he had less than two weeks before the season began. **Tracy McGrath**

Lawrence Lewis was Jeremy's best man at his wedding and even lived with McGrath at his Canyon Lake, California, home. **Tracy McGrath**

Normally, factory teams spend four months testing before the start of the season, but Jeremy only had ten days. He had only been riding Suzukis for 45 days and was still adapting. One of the biggest challenges facing Jeremy was the fact that Suzuki didn't have a huge war chest of works parts, or a giant in-house machine shop to fabricate specialty items. By all accounts, Suzuki didn't outlay as much money as Honda did on its racing effort. Roger DeCoster spent a lot of time at Pro Circuit on their dyno working with Mitch Payton on the horsepower issue. Jeremy demanded more usable power and torque, and DeCoster and Payton were focused on giving it to him.

McGrath also hated the conventional Showa fork because it flexed too much at his speed. He couldn't trust it on technical tracks where engineered flex wasn't as important as it was with high-speed outdoor tracks. Jeremy tested a fork brace, but it didn't solve the problem. He tried thicker triple clamps with a three pinch-bolt design and didn't like that either.

When the series headed to Daytona Beach, many expected Jeremy to suffer. But he pulled off a solid third, which was par for the course, considering he had only won Daytona once during his previous three visits. The conventional fork favored the track design, so it didn't hinder Jeremy like it did on normal supercross tracks.

That week, McGrath knew he had to do something about the front suspension. He still owned a practice Honda, and he took off the front fork and had triple clamps built for his works RM250. He also used the works Nissan brake system off the CR250 because he didn't like the feel of the works Suzuki system and he felt it faded under too much use.

The next week in Minneapolis, he got his first win with the new setup. This broke the longest losing streak of McGrath's 250cc career and renewed his confidence in himself and the bike.

"We were all relieved when Jeremy got his first win," Harris says. "Suzuki had the most to lose and the least to gain. Everyone knew that Jeremy was the fastest rider in 1996. If he won on Suzukis, then everyone would assume it was Jeremy. But if he lost the title, we knew everyone would blame the bikes. But we had to do something to turn our race program around, and Jeremy definitely helped with the development and image of our race program."

Jeremy followed with a third in Houston, a second in Orlando, and another victory in St. Louis. It was apparent that the lack of testing had dramatically affected Jeremy's results. All the other teams and riders had finished their testing in January, when MC was just beginning. Had it not been for clutch problems and a wimpy fork, Jeremy would have been competitive. Rumors started to surface that McGrath wanted to retire. He didn't look like the same McGrath who had won the last four championships, and he didn't fully trust his bike.

Jeremy was down by nine points to Team Kawasaki's Jeff Emig. Emig had come into his own since winning his first supercross in 1996 when the lights went out in Las Vegas. Jeremy placed fourth in Pontiac, although he should have won—he led for 18 laps before going over the bars in a corner. Fortunately for MC, Emig finished seventh and Jeremy was able to cut the points lead even further.

A week later the series headed to Charlotte with McGrath only two points behind Emig. He was doing well in North Carolina until he got a flat rear tire. That held him to seventh place and hurt his championship hopes even more.

Jeremy spent the next week at Guy Cooper's private moto playground in Stillwater, Oklahoma. His best friend, Lawrence Lewis, drove bikes out from

Team Kawasaki's Jeff Emig became the first rider to stop Jeremy's run of supercross championships. **Ken Faught/Dirt Rider**

The uncertainty of McGrath's predicament was apparent right from the beginning, but his move would allow salaries to creep up during the coming years. **Tracy McGrath**

McGrath faced tough questions from reporters, including Leanne Tweeden, once it became apparent that he was no longer the fastest rider. **Dirt Rider**

Hole shots were rare for Jeremy and his Suzuki, but he did grab the early lead here at Budds Creek in Maryland. **Dirt Rider**

California for the filming of *Steel Roots*. Jeremy and Lew own Clutch Films and wanted to make their own extreme video. Jimmy Button, Grayson Goodman, and I spent three days at Cooperland and a nearby public track that Cooper calls "The 500." It turned out to be one of the most historic free-ride sessions of all time and produced one of the bestselling videos to date.

Jeremy managed to jump an uphill triple, land on elevated flat ground, and ride a wheelie for 150 feet before the front wheel touched ground. There was a huge uphill step-up jump that Jeremy and Jimmy stared at for a half-hour while Cooper made other jumps with his tractor. Cooper came over, asked them why they were nervous, and then hit the big gap on his Husaberg

501cc four-stroke. Button and McGrath were so shocked that they were almost embarrassed. After all, Cooper was retired, and Jeremy was battling for the supercross points lead. A few minutes later, they both jumped it, despite their nervousness.

Emig won the next event in Dallas while Jeremy finished fourth. This was the first time since becoming a factory rider that it looked like he might actually lose a stadium title. Emig's points lead had grown once again. In order for Jeremy to win the title, he had to win Las Vegas and Emig had to finish sixth or worse.

Just when Jeremy had to suck up the pressure and pull off one of the biggest upsets in supercross history, the unexpected happened. While screwing around with a bunch of friends at a restaurant, the champ stepped on a broken beer bottle and sliced his Achilles' tendon. He had to have eight stitches which meant that Jeremy would have to ride injured once again.

Over time, McGrath adapted to the Suzuki, but he felt Yamaha had the best bikes for the 1998 season. **Karel Kramer/Dirt Rider**

After the Charlotte supercross in North Carolina, McGrath went to Guy Cooper's house in Stillwater, Oklahoma, to tape *Steel Roots.* **Ken Faught/Dirt Rider**

Guy Cooper tried to chase down McGrath, but even the home track advantage couldn't stop the kid nicknamed Showtime. **Ken Faught/Dirt Rider**

The *Steel Roots* video is full of in-your-face action and is considered one of the best off-road motorcycling videos. After all, it was produced by the same people who created the cult classic *Crusty Demons of Dirt*. **Ken Faught/Dirt Rider**

When the race in Las Vegas finally rolled around, it was apparent that Jeremy wasn't up to speed. The foot throbbed, but MC gave it his all. In the end, Emig finished fourth and Jeremy came in seventh. That night, 26-year-old Jeff Emig became the oldest champ in SX history, and Jeremy suffered his first loss.

"I really couldn't believe it at the time," says McGrath. "I just had a lot of freak things happen that year that had never happened to me before. I really think I could have won the title on the Suzuki if we had more testing time. The bike eventually came around, and even though it wasn't a Honda, it was still okay. I proved that I could win on it. I always wonder what would have happened if I didn't get taken out by Lamson, get the flat, or cut my heal. That stuff always bothers me, but there's nothing I could do about it now."

Jeremy didn't have much luck in the 1997 outdoor series either. His best finish was at the season opener in Gainesville, Florida, where he was runner-up. He placed third a handful of times and no worse than eighth during the 12 rounds. In the end, he really wasn't competitive and completed the series third overall.

At the end of the season, Jeremy wasn't convinced that Suzuki's race program had what he needed to win against a group of well-funded manufacturers. For Suzuki, however, this proved to be a good thing. The problems facing McGrath forced Suzuki to build a full-blown state-of-the-art race shop, with a high-end machine shop. Suzuki's new setup was arguably better than Honda's, but for McGrath, it was too little, too late.

Although Jeremy insists that he would have stayed with Suzuki had he won the supercross title, he went looking for a new deal, and it proved once again to be a big surprise.

Above: Cliff climbing is a big part of riding at Cooperland, and crashes like this were common. **Ken Faught/Dirt Rider**

Above, left: Jimmy Button, along with Grayson Goodman, flew back to Cooper's house to add some style to Jeremy's first attempt at video making. **Ken Faught/Dirt Rider**

Left: McGrath's surgically precise style is what allowed him to race so long with so few injuries. **Ken Faught/Dirt Rider**

71

Next Stop, Yamaha

Jeremy and Chaparral Form the Blue Brigade

At the end of Jeremy's one-year contract with Suzuki, he called me and asked to borrow a few of

our test bikes. He knew that all of the manufacturers flew in first-run production machines for *Dirt*

Rider to test, and McGrath trusted us not to let anyone know what he was doing. I loaned him our

1998 Yamaha YZ250 and Honda CR250. He wouldn't consider going back to Honda, but I think he wanted to

get an idea how things had evolved with the second-generation aluminum frame.

McGrath's creation of Chaparral Yamaha Team in 1998 suited him perfectly. He was consistently on the podium and scored his first win at round four in the Seattle Kingdome. He reeled off a string of victories after that and won the title comfortably despite a few lackluster finishes through the close of the season. **Ken Faught/Dirt Rider**

Jeremy was leaning toward racing Yamahas, but knew he had his choice of manufacturers. In 1997, Jimmy Button worked a deal with Team Chaparral to ride YZs full-time and moved into Jeremy's Canyon Lake, California, home. Button told Chaparral team manager Larry Brooks that Jeremy was looking for a new home for 1998. Brooks approached Dave Damron with the idea and the owner of Chaparral made it happen. Jeremy's base salary was $500,000, plus money from other sponsors like Fox Racing, Alpinestars, Bell Helmets, and Spy Optics, and he would have the same factory bikes as Kevin Windham and Doug Henry.

The King of Supercross won three more titles after he signed with Yamaha, eventually bringing his career total to seven. **Ken Faught/Dirt Rider**

Yamaha, however, didn't want to relinquish control of its factory hardware. They didn't want to let works parts and technology out of their sight, so they insisted on hiring the mechanic for MC instead of letting Chaparral take on the responsibilities. The lack of trust complicated matters, but it was the law of the land at the time.

Skip Norfolk had helped Jeremy out during his last few months at Suzuki, but he didn't want to spin wrenches full-time. Randy Lawrence was hired as MC's team mechanic. Randy's brother Phil was a Yamaha support rider, and the two had been friends with Jeremy for years.

"I was at a turning point with our race team when we found out that Jeremy wanted to ride for Chaparral," Damron says. "I was tired of racing for seventh place. We either had to go big or go home. The race team is a very important part of our business and it plays an important role in the image of Chaparral. By hiring the world's most popular rider and going head-to-head with the factories, it made a statement. It showed that we took our racing serious, and we tried to give Jeremy everything he needed to start winning again. A lot of people doubted him at first, but he's a champion, and we had a lot of faith in his abilities. Win or lose, Chaparral would be considered a player with McGrath on our team."

Always the trendsetter, MC got these custom Alpinestars boots in 2001. **Ken Faught/Dirt Rider**

The No Fear MX line of apparel was partially owned by McGrath, and soon Jeremy had to sponsor some of his own competitors including Travis Pastrana, Kevin Windham, and Sebastien Tortelli. **Ken Faught/Dirt Rider**

Above: From 1993 until 2003, Jeremy was a fixture during opening ceremonies at every supercross. **Ken Faught/Dirt Rider**

Above right: The fireworks show during supercross can really be loud for those standing in the middle of the action. **Ken Faught/Dirt Rider**

With the new team, Jeremy found more inspiration and renewed confidence. He vowed to focus on his testing efforts with Yamaha and not suffer the same problems that he encountered with the last-minute switch to Suzuki. He was much more prepared and familiar with his bike going into the season opener at the Los Angeles Memorial Coliseum. Although it was a mud race, Jeremy finished third behind first-time winner Sebastien Tortelli.

"That was a very special night for me," Tortelli says. "There is always a lot of talk about the first race of the season, and most of the talk was about McGrath on Yamahas. He usually started the season off really strong, so for me to beat him at a time he was trying to prove himself all over again, was really cool."

He followed that up with a second in Houston and another runner-up in Tempe. Jeff Emig wasn't on his A-game, but McGrath realized Ezra Lusk was the new title threat. The Georgian had signed with Team Honda and was riding better than he had at any point earlier in his career.

Jeremy came back to win Seattle and then San Diego. He was riding incredibly well and looked like he could regain the title. The 1998 win in San Diego was McGrath's 64th career win and made him the all-time leader for combined supercross and motocross AMA wins. He scored win number 65 in Indy and number 66 in Atlanta. McGrath crashed in Tampa and finished eighth, but then cleaned house on the sands of Daytona Beach, which had traditionally been his biggest weakness. Jeremy finished second in New Orleans and won Minneapolis before heading into St. Louis.

"We were really relieved when Jeremy started winning on Yamahas," Brooks says. "Honda and Kawasaki were the teams to beat at the time, and Jeremy was slowly returning to his 1996 championship form. It was great to be part of the whole Chaparral deal."

MC had another epic battle with Lusk. The two riders collided at the end of the race and both went down. Lusk got up to claim the final podium spot, and Jeremy finished a disappointing fourth. The crash created a lot of bad blood between the two and renewed Jeremy's frustration and anger toward Honda.

MC at speed. **Ken Faught/Dirt Rider**

Throughout his career, McGrath had more gear combinations than any other factory rider in history. **Ken Faught/Dirt Rider**

McGrath had a supercross-only contract with Yamaha but still raced a few Nationals for fun. **Dirt Rider**

Jeremy takes in the moment with his parents, Jack and Ann, and sister Tracy. **Ken Faught/Dirt Rider**

The next race, in Pontiac, Michigan, was one of the most memorable races of Jeremy's career. It marked one of the biggest public crashes for the three-time champ, who appeared to be on course to reclaiming the No. 1 plate. After landing from a jump, the triple clamp snapped and Jeremy flipped over the bars. As he got up, he caught Larry Ward's elbow and went down again. This was the only time in Jeremy's career that he didn't finish a supercross. In fact, with the exception of Las Vegas in 1996 when the lights went out, McGrath had never missed a supercross. Jeremy didn't realize it at the time, but he got a concussion and had broken the navicular bone in his wrist. It's the smallest bone in the body and can cause death if blood flow gets restricted.

Jeremy rode injured in Charlotte and earned seven championship points with a 14th overall. The following race in Dallas would give Jeremy the 1998 title if he could place second or better. Although he was still riding in a lot of pain, he managed to trail Lusk across the finish line. For the fourth time in his career, Jeremy was the supercross champion, and proved to everyone that he was back and ready for more.

He capped the season with a win in Las Vegas and then started the AMA 250cc National Championship with a second at Glen Helen. Jeremy was on fire and wanted the world to know it. His first outdoor win on a Yamaha came in round two in Hangtown where he picked up the series points lead. He followed that up with a sixth in Mt. Morris and then broke his wrist. This meant he would miss the remaining nine rounds, but he still finished 14th in the series.

At the end of the season, Jeremy was looking at a whole new program for 1999. He was tired of racing outdoors and had an opportunity with long-time friend Jeff Surwall to start a new gear company with licensing from No Fear. Jeremy's relationship with Fox Racing had deteriorated; his contract would be void if he changed his program. The supercross-only deal would do that.

At the end of the year, Jeremy went out on a photo shoot with Donn Maeda, the editor of *MXracer*, a magazine Donn and I started with Tom Webb and Bob Weber. According to Jeremy, Maeda promised not

Chaparral, the world's largest motorcycle dealership, was the one who lured McGrath away from Suzuki. They bought a semi, hired Larry Brooks as a team manager, teamed Jeremy with close friend Jimmy Button, and went racing full-time. At a time when some were wondering if Jeremy would retire after losing on Suzukis, the Yamaha deal rekindled the fire of the aging champion. **Ken Faught/Dirt Rider**

to use the photos in an issue until the beginning of the new year. Jeremy says he stressed to Donn that it would cause him problems with Fox.

The photos appeared in the December issue of *MXracer*. Fox was upset about the entire situation, though they knew Jeremy was leaving the team. Ann McGrath called my house on Christmas Eve with a bunch of questions. She knew I was in an awkward position and had nothing to do with the current situation, but Fox reportedly still owed Jeremy $220,000 of his $320,000 salary, and now they didn't want to pay. The McGraths explored all of their options, but ultimately decided to cut their losses and aggressively pursue opportunities with No Fear.

In contrast to his career, Jeremy's social life was calming down. Buddy and Shelly Antunez introduced him to Kim Maddox, and McGrath took the relationship seriously. At the end of the season, he sold his Canyon Lake home and purchased a 6000-square-foot estate in Encinitas, California. Kim moved in with him, and at 28, Jeremy started looking at life a little differently. He added a huge shop, gym, tennis court, and a rock pool.

Jeremy rolled into 1999 with a whole new look with the No Fear gear. Despite a seventh-place finish at the season opener in Anaheim, his worst finish of the season, he was still in championship form. McGrath battled most of the season with Ezra Lusk and finished on the podium all but four times. He won eight times, finished runner-up on four occasions, and never placed third. McGrath earned his sixth title in a historical year that extended many of his records.

"During this time Jeremy found his confidence once again," Damron says. "He was really happy with the bikes and was strong both physically and mentally."

Jeremy raced two AMA 250cc Nationals even though they weren't in his contract. He placed tenth

McGrath won 72 supercross main events during his career, an accomplishment that may never be beaten. **Ken Faught/ Dirt Rider**

Once Chaparral decided to stop racing, McGrath funded his entire team. He bought a half-million-dollar semi, worked out a deal with Yamaha to get works bikes and salary, and then attacked the 16-race series. **Ken Faught/Dirt Rider**

The champ was always looking for new and innovative lines and was always one of the most focused racers during practice. **Ken Faught/Dirt Rider**

Very few people could ever keep up with McGrath, but on several occasions Doug Henry managed to give Jeremy a run for his money. **Scott Hoffman/Dirt Rider**

Heading into the 2005 supercross series, it doesn't look like anyone will catch McGrath's record of 72 250cc main event wins. Ricky Carmichael is the closest at 33, while Ricky Johnson has 28 and Bob Hannah has 27. **Ken Faught/ Dirt Rider**

at Glen Helen and eighth at Washougal. He was looking for more control over his racing program and wanted to up his game. After months of planning, McGrath started his own team and lured Skip Norfolk back to spin wrenches. He spent a half-million dollars on his own semi and created Team McGrath Racing/Mazda/Yamaha. Jeremy also hired Larry Brooks as team manager, and when the group debuted at Anaheim, McGrath was literally the talk of the town.

"This was a business decision on both sides," Damron says. "There wasn't much more that Chaparral could accomplish with Jeremy. We already proved that we could be competitive at the highest level, and Jeremy felt like there were more opportunities out there if he ran his own program. We backed out of racing for a while until 2003 when we got involved with Kevin Windham, Mike LaRocco, and the Factory Connection/Amsoil team."

"Jeremy just wanted to do something different," Jack McGrath says. "He had been able to put together some of his own personal deals with Suzuki and Chaparral, but he thought he could take the sport to the next level if he could have control over the entire thing. He knew this was a big deal, and he knew there were a lot of risks involved. I give him a lot of credit because he had to deal with all of that pressure when he could have taken the normal factory rider route and had things easy. But Jeremy has never been about making things easier on himself. That's what's made him a champion. With his own team, he had to pay for all of the expenses and he had to worry about a bunch of employees.

McGrath won the first two rounds of the 2000 season, both at Edison Field, and then he suffered a serious blow in San Diego. During Saturday's practice, Jimmy Button crashed hard on his big-bore Yamaha four-stroke even though it was at low speed. When Jimmy's mom walked down to the field, she looked frustrated that Jimmy was hurt this early in the season and thought it would be a simple broken bone or torn ligament. She was devastated when she got the news that Jimmy had no feeling in his legs.

"He's one of the cleanest racers of all time. I always knew that I could trust him no matter what. When he was in his prime, he knew he could beat anyone in the world during heads-up racing, so he didn't have to do anything funny. As a racer, that's really important, and I will always have a lot of respect forwhat he accomplished in this sport. He is and always will be the King of Supercross."

—Greg Albertyn, Three-time World MX Champion and 1999 AMA 250cc National Champion

Button went to Sharps, a well-known trauma center in San Diego. Two weeks later, he was moved to Barrow's Neurological Center in Phoenix to be near his parents. He spent a long time in rehabilitation, and fortunately, he's able to walk now, though it's with a limp.

Mentally, Button's accident was tough for Jeremy to handle. He placed fourth in San Diego as Ricky Carmichael won his second race of his 250 career aboard a Kawasaki. After dominating

For a while, McGrath worked with Gary Semics on riding technique. Here the two discuss Yamaha's private test track in Corona, California. **Ken Faught/ Dirt Rider**

125s for several years, RC was really starting to get up to speed in the premiere class.

Jeremy won seven of the first ten races and was still viewed as the rider to beat. He went on to win in Michigan, Illinois, and Nevada. For the seventh time in eight years, Jeremy was the AMA Supercross Champ.

"I was having a lot of fun racing, and thought I was invincible," says McGrath. "I knew I couldn't keep it up forever, but I was definitely enjoying the moment."

At the same time, Ricky Carmichael was becoming an all-around rider. He took his training more seriously and was determined to come out of the gate harder than ever.

Jeremy scored victories two out of the first three rounds in 2001, but then it became a Carmichael show. Jeremy finished no worse than sixth (once in Daytona Beach and once in Salt Lake City), but he suffered his second championship loss. At the end of 2001, Jeremy finished second in points, and Kawasaki's Ricky Carmichael was the new champ.

"I knew Carmichael was fast, but I didn't think he would have the consistency to be a

McGrath held the all-time record for wins in 125cc supercross until James Stewart shattered the record in 2004. **Ken Faught/Dirt Rider**

No intimidation here…McGrath and Carmichael make small talk during the opening ceremonies at Anaheim Stadium in January 2001. **Ken Faught/Dirt Rider**

During his career, McGrath was always the last rider introduced, and he always drew the loudest cheers. **Scott Hoffman/Dirt Rider**

McGrath's biggest strength was his confidence. He would engineer a hole shot at most races, and then run a sprint race for five to seven laps until the other riders literally gave up. He was so fast that many people felt like they were racing for second. **Ken Faught/Dirt Rider**

Ricky Carmichael beat MC at Daytona in 2000, but that was almost expected. Daytona was the champ's least favorite supercross because of its high speeds and deep sand. Carmichael was used to the conditions because he grew up in Florida riding under the same conditions. **Mark Kariya/Dirt Rider**

champ," says McGrath. "He had a reputation for riding over his head, and after a while, I kind of sat back and waited for a mistake. I didn't want him to take both of us out, and I didn't want to get hurt. In the end, I waited too long before I made my move."

Many critics said that Jeremy had become too relaxed with his training regimen and lost focus. Others claimed he was starting to show the effects of not racing year-round. Jeremy's supercross-only contract meant that he was only racing 16 times a year, plus select overseas events. Other racers, like Ricky Carmichael were racing 28–32 races each year.

McGrath spent the off-season training harder than ever before. He spent more time testing and was hungry for the elusive title number eight.

"Jeremy doesn't like getting beat," Jack McGrath says. "He didn't like it when Emig beat him in 1997 and he liked it even worse when RC took his crown. It was kind of difficult to be around Jeremy at this time. He was very frustrated, and I started noticing some changes in his personality. He began to really look at life differently, and I could see that he wanted to win more than ever. He stepped up his training, spent more time testing, and worked really hard on his starts."

Above, left: McGrath won 26 races on Yamahas while he won 44 on Hondas and two on Suzukis. **Dirt Rider**

Above, right: McGrath celebrates his first championship on Yamahas as a member of Team Chaparral in 1998. **Ken Faught/Dirt Rider**

Left: McGrath ran this American flag on the back of his helmet at Anaheim in 1999. **Ken Faught/Dirt Rider**

After wrapping up the championship in 1998, mechanic Randy Lawrence scratches out the No. 2 on the front number plate. **Ken Faught/Dirt Rider**

One of the main ingredients for McGrath's success was good equipment. When he rode for Honda and Yamaha, there wasn't a better machine on the track, and that gave him a lot of confidence. **Ken Faught/Dirt Rider**

McGrath is of the founding partners in Spy, a goggle and sunglasses manufacturer started in the mid-1990s. **Ken Faught/Dirt Rider**

This is one of only three times McGrath won Daytona during his career. He won in 1996, 1998, and 1999. **Ken Faught/ Dirt Rider**

When the 2002 season kicked off in Anaheim, however, it was very apparent that something was wrong with Jeremy. He placed 13th during round one, followed by tenth and ninth in San Diego and Anaheim II. It was by far the worst start to a season in Jeremy's career, and he had a new opponent called arm pump.

"I don't know what's going on," McGrath said at the time. "I never had a problem with arm pump during my entire career. I'm doing everything I can, but it seems like I'm fighting an uphill battle."

While Jeremy was struggling, things at Team Honda weren't much better. Carmichael took a nasty header at the season opener and was hit hard by Mike LaRocco. The crash knocked out the defending champ, sending RC to nearby UCI Medical Center and leaving him with a single point.

After a few rounds, word on the street was that McGrath had over-trained. He tried all sorts of quick remedies, but nothing worked. It took him eight rounds to make his first podium—a third in Atlanta. Although the second half of the season was better, he only placed third four times and never finished any higher. Jeremy McGrath was completely shut out, and this was the first and only season that he didn't win a single race.

"I was definitely bummed at this point," says McGrath. "The season is so short that you can't fix things in time. Once you realize you have a problem, you're too far into the series, especially when other guys are having a good year. I still had a lot of confidence and felt like I could still win. I hate losing races, but I hate losing championships even more. I finished the year in third, and I wanted to improve things in 2003."

At the end of the season, Jeremy expected to renew his contract with Yamaha and then planned to retire. Unfortunately for Jeremy, Yamaha was in the process of signing Australian Chad Reed. When McGrath sat down at the negotiation table, Yamaha offered him $300,000 and a one-year deal. Jeremy had made $750,000 the year before, so he went shopping for a new ride.

McGrath ran a No. 12 sticker on his radiator shroud and helmet in honor of his close friend Jimmy Button who was temporarily paralyzed from a racing accident at the San Diego supercross. **Ken Faught/Dirt Rider**

McGrath could stay low on jumps because he had the ability to suck the bike up to his chest on takeoff. This prevented the suspension effect from catapulting him higher and further. Essentially, he could hit the jump faster and avoid over-jumping an obstacle by using this technique. **Ken Faught/Dirt Rider**

In May 1999, McGrath dyed his hair blue after winning the SX title for a second year on Yamahas. All of the press, including Enrico Borghi from the Italian magazine *Moto Sprint*, burned lots of film on MC's new color. **Ken Faught/Dirt Rider**

McGrath's first season without scoring a win came in 2002. **Ken Faught/Dirt Rider**

Randy Lawrence only worked with McGrath for a short time before McGrath Racing managed to lure Skip Norfolk back as a full-time mechanic. Norfolk now works wrenches for Team Kawasaki. **Ken Faught/Dirt Rider**

Riders get less than one hour of practice on the track before race day; they need to make the most of their limited time. **Ken Faught/Dirt Rider**

McGrath's ability to get to the first turn with the lead was incredible, and nothing could have hurt his competition more. **Ken Faught/Dirt Rider**

The King and his crown. **Ken Faught/Dirt Rider**

McGrath finished second in the 2001 championship and then slipped to third in 2002, the worst finish of his amazing career. **Ken Faught/Dirt Rider**

McGrath's last career victory came at the second Anaheim race in 2001. **Ken Faught/Dirt Rider**

McGrath really never let anything bother him, at least nothing that he let anyone know about. He was always remarkably calm and didn't get caught up in the head games that some of the riders tried to play. He was friends with most of the riders, like Kevin Windham, himself a supercross winner. **Ken Faught/ Dirt Rider**

No single rider has been photographed more than Jeremy McGrath. The trained eye can tell that two camera flashes have hit McGrath at the exact same moment as evident by the highlights coming from his right-hand side. **Ken Faught/Dirt Rider**

Even when McGrath didn't win, he often posted the fastest lap times of the night. **Ken Faught/Dirt Rider**

Outdoor races offer a different type of challenge because the courses are rougher and the terrain is less consistent. **Ken Faught/Dirt Rider**

McGrath rarely used hand guards and you'll only see them on his bike when it was muddy or rocky. **Scott Hoffman/ Dirt Rider**

The Washougal course in Washington is one of the fastest tracks on the AMA circuit. **Scott Hoffman/Dirt Rider**

McGrath gave his all at every race, and that's what made him a champion. **Mark Kariya/Dirt Rider**

Above: Some of his Nac-Nacs, like this one in Indianapolis, were pure insanity. There has arguably never been a cooler trick thrown at a supercross. **Dirt Rider**

Above, right: McGrath sported the No. 02 for the 2000 Glen Helen National, a style usually seen on the All-Japan Nationals. **Ken Faught/Dirt Rider**

Right: McGrath ended his racing career without ever racing a four-stroke in motocross or supercross. **Ken Faught/Dirt Rider**

McGrath had several strengths, including excellent starts, an amazing technique through whoops, and the ability to take tight inside lines. **Ken Faught/Dirt Rider**

Jeremy's worldwide success attracted a lot of outside sponsors, like Mazda, which you see branded across his chest.
Ken Faught/Dirt Rider

The King's bike and his roadside castle. **Ken Faught/Dirt Rider**

McGrath loved Glen Helen because it was only 30 minutes from where he grew up in Southern California. **Ken Faught/ Dirt Rider**

Jeremy always said that he was racing for fun and for the fans. He knew if he could win races and entertain, then the money would come later. He proved he wasn't racing for the money when he backed out of a multi-million-dollar deal once he realized he was no longer competitive. **Ken Faught/Dirt Rider**

New Zealander Shane King picks up some pointers from McGrath before the start of the 2000 Indy supercross. **Ken Faught/Dirt Rider**

Pontiac, Michigan, in 1998 was the only time in McGrath's career that he didn't finish a supercross main event. He crashed over a triple jump and snapped the triple clamp clean off. Little did he know, Jeremy also broke the navicular in his wrist, the smallest bone in the human body. He rode in a lot of pain the next week in Charlotte and struggled to finish 14th. Incredibly enough, McGrath had such a big point lead that he still won the championship and managed to pull off a win less than a month after his most famous crash. **Scott Hoffman/Dirt Rider**

Shots of Jeremy starting in second are rare. If you look closely at this photo, you can see Ryan Hughes crashing in the background. **Ken Faught/Dirt Rider**

McGrath is the most adored supercross rider of all time. **Ken Faught/Dirt Rider**

McGrath had a unique style of cornering in bowl turns. He would actually sit toward the back of his seat and steer with the throttle. Once Ricky Carmichael adapted to the style, he started beating MC. **Ken Faught/ Dirt Rider**

Practice, practice, practice is what made McGrath so good at starts. **Ken Faught/Dirt Rider**

Notice that Jeremy's front wheel is sucked under the front fender and completely bottomed out. The champ had a knack for pushing his equipment to the edge. **Ken Faught/Dirt Rider**

Carmichael switched to Honda, but proved to be his own worst enemy on 250s. **Ken Faught/Dirt Rider**

McGrath stands in the kitchen of his estate in Encinitas, California. **Ken Faught/Dirt Rider**

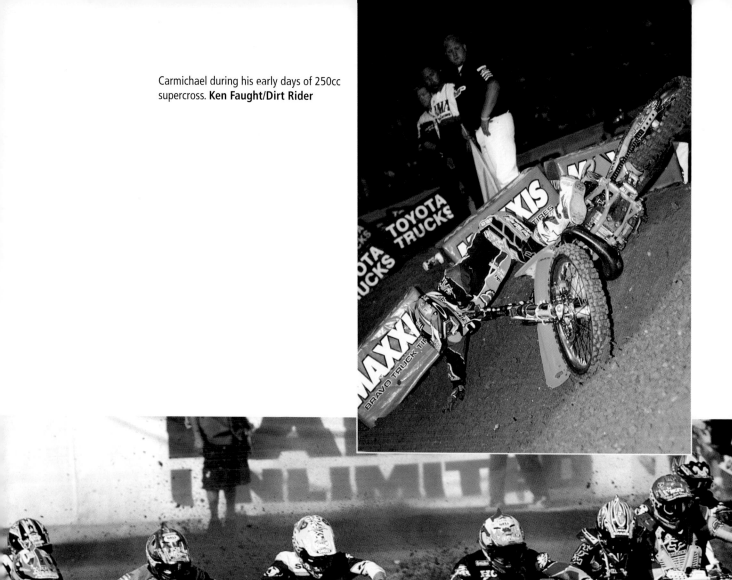

Carmichael during his early days of 250cc supercross. **Ken Faught/Dirt Rider**

McGrath gets sandwiched by Ricky Carmichael (No. 4) and Greg Albertyn (No. 1) at the start of the Glen Helen National in 2000. **Ken Faught/Dirt Rider**

Once Ricky Carmichael learned to slow down in order to go fast, he was tough to beat. When he won in 2001, he became the second rider in history to beat McGrath during a supercross championship. **Ken Faught/Dirt Rider**

McGrath's Yamahas may not have looked as high-tech as some of the other bikes, but that's because most of the secrets were hidden inside. **Ken Faught/Dirt Rider**

Chapter Seven

The KTM Deal

The King Steps Aside

Midway through the 2002 season, it became apparent that things were falling apart between Yamaha and McGrath Racing. Even from the outside it was clear that Yamaha's factory racing team viewed Jeremy McGrath as a competitor, not as a member of the corporate family.

"It didn't really feel like I had their support anymore," McGrath says. "Around some of the guys it even felt like they enjoyed watching me lose. It was really odd and frustrating."

When KTM did the deal with Jeremy McGrath, it shook up the motocross community. During the onset of McGrath's career, the Austrian company wasn't very well known in the United States, and his deal immediately elevated the manufacturer's status. Although McGrath never raced a KTM in supercross, the team won the 2003 AMA 125cc National Championship with Grant Langston, who spent much of the season battling with teammate Ryan Hughes. **Ken Faught/Dirt Rider**

During my daughter Hannah's birthday party in March, Jeremy and I met in my home office with my father-in-law, Mel Harris. Jeremy explained that things weren't headed in the right direction. Word had already leaked out that Chad Reed was signing with Yamaha, and the manufacturer had chosen the Australian to be its new hired gun. Jeremy still had an offer on the table, but it was less than half of what he made in 2002. Mel was trying to figure out what to do with Suzuki's motocross team. He was frustrated with Travis Pastrana and was looking for a change. They talked numbers for about half an hour, and then we joined the rest of the birthday party in the backyard.

A few months passed and I saw Jeremy at the Mammoth Mountain Motocross race in June. My wife Amy, daughter Hannah, and I walked into Jeremy's Weekend Warrior trailer, closed the door, and started talking about the coming year. I told Jeremy that Mel wanted him, but Roger DeCoster and Hide Suzaki did not. Roger was the team manager, Hide was his boss, and Mel put a lot of trust in their opinions. Roger and Hide didn't believe that Jeremy could win anymore and felt a new deal wouldn't be good for the long-term health of the team. Although Greg Albertyn won the AMA 250cc National Championship in 1999 with Suzuki, the boys in yellow were still battling their reputation of being sub-par to Honda and Yamaha. They felt Jeremy was at the end of his career and didn't want to invest too much in someone who would retire in the near future.

McGrath's personality and style elevated the sport of supercross to what it is today. He drew in outside sponsors who now fund many of the 28 semi-trucks that create a makeshift community called the pits. **Massimo Melani/Dirt Rider**

McGrath was responsible for every aspect of his team. He had the pressure of dealing with every sponsor and knowing that his employees depended on him for their livelihood. **Ken Faught/ Dirt Rider**

Classic MC style at Barona Oaks in Southern California. **Ken Faught/Dirt Rider**

During a phone conversation with Ann McGrath, she commented, "Pretty soon, people won't be talking about how he's riding, they'll be talking about what he's riding."

While in Mammoth, Jeremy played a round of golf with Ron Heben. Heben was a factory mechanic for Yamaha and Honda, served as team manager for Suzuki and Kawasaki's Team Green, and was now in charge of KTM's race effort. Few people knew it at the time, but Jeremy was in serious talks with the Austrian company. Things died down with Suzuki, but he was also exploring his options with Kawasaki.

By the time Jeremy's wedding rolled around on August 3, there were all sorts of rumors circulating. Some said Jeremy would ride green for 2003; others said he signed a KTM contract while sipping coffee at Starbucks. In reality, Jeremy had made up his mind, but wouldn't say what he was doing.

Meanwhile, KTM hired Ryan Hughes to help testing. Hughes retired from racing a year earlier, but missed the excitement and wanted to get back on a bike. Hughes helped convince Jeremy that KTM was a viable option, and within a short time, Jeremy told the world about his new deal. It was perhaps the biggest news of the year, but no one could have anticipated the incredible chain of events that followed.

With few 2003 KTMs in the country, Jeremy knew that testing would be important. He wasn't sure that a small company like KTM could work fast enough to give him competitive equipment, but he loved the production motor. He claimed it was as fast as, or faster than, his works Yamaha and set out to test with mechanic Skip Norfolk. Soon, McGrath realized that there were problems with the rear suspension. KTM is the only manufacturer that runs a link-less shock and Jeremy had difficulties with handling. He tried a bunch of things, including a triple clamp offset, and made some headway, but had concerns about the overall competitiveness.

This was a hectic time. Most of the photos that exist of Jeremy on a KTM came during a last-minute photo session at Barona Oaks, a track in San Diego. Eric Johnson interviewed MC for *Racer X* and I did the same for *Dirt Rider* and Speed Channel. With all the hype and enthusiasm, it looked as though Jeremy was re-energized and on a mission to prove something to Yamaha.

"I was surprised when I found out that Jeremy signed with KTM," Ricky Carmichael says. "It sounded pretty farfetched at first, but once I knew it was true, I figured that Jeremy knew what he was doing. He had never been about the money, so I figured their new bike was really good. A lot of people asked me whether or not I thought it was a good move, and I would tell them that I would never count Jeremy out. He's won a lot of titles, and I knew he didn't like being beat."

ESPN's Jamie Little interviewed Jeremy in the pits at Anaheim. After this event, the half-million-dollar semi was never seen again at a professional race.
Ken Faught/Dirt Rider

On September 21, 2002, while testing at KTM's private test track in Corona a short time later, Jeremy's bike bogged on the face of a triple jump and ejected him over the handlebar. According to McGrath, he was testing fuel tanks when a check valve on a vent hose was accidentally put in backwards. Although the accident was preventable, it left Jeremy on the ground in severe pain. The top of his right femur popped out of the hip socket and his future began to look questionable. Jeremy spent a painful evening in the hospital as doctors tried to replace the dis-jointed limb. After putting him out, it took four doctors to get the femur back in his hip socket.

A couple weeks later, my family and I hooked up with McGrath at Stefan Elvyn's house in Perris, California. Stefan runs an international motocross camp for aspiring racers and thought it would be cool for Jeremy to drop by the compound and surprise the dozen or so kids from overseas.

Although I had talked to him on the phone, it was the first time I had seen Jeremy walk since the accident. It was apparent that it was bothering him more than he wanted his com-petitors to know. Stefan and I walked out to his shop for a half-hour, and when we came back into the house, I saw a pretty odd sight. Jeremy was at the kitchen counter coloring with my daughter while 17 guys between the ages of 16 and 28 watched. These guys had the world's greatest motorcycle racer in the house and they had no questions for him. Granted, they didn't speak English well, but they just sat at the dining room table watching every move the pair made with their Crayolas.

"I don't like seeing anyone hurt, but I knew it would affect Jeremy in one way or another," Carmichael says. "Even if your body recovers 100 percent, it will still affect you mentally. Every

McGrath loved the KTM power, but could never come to grips with the way the rear suspension worked.
Ken Faught/Dirt Rider

Few people ever got to see McGrath ride a KTM, and even fewer got to see him do tricks like this live. This photo was taken on the same day Thor did their ads with the King. **Ken Faught/Dirt Rider**

time you hit a tricky jump or something you don't feel totally comfortable with, you start worrying about crashing again. And when it's a mechanical problem, you worry even more."

When Jeremy started to feel better, he decided to head overseas to check his speed and things took another nasty turn. Jeremy collided with Kyle Lewis over a triple jump and went down hard. The impact left the seven-time SX champ laying on the track unconscious. Although he escaped serious injury, he says the accident robbed him of his confidence.

"Jeremy's really never been hurt that much in his career," DeCoster says. "For him to have two big accidents this close together was probably a wake-up call for him. No matter what, it had to hurt his confidence."

In December, Jeremy called me to see if he could get permission to ride in the field across the street from his parent's shop where we rode as kids. The property was now fenced in and owned by Danny Carlson's future in-laws. Danny is one of my key test riders at *Dirt Rider*. Jeremy asked me to call him, but I thought it would be best if Jeremy did it himself. Naturally, they gave McGrath permission and met him at the home-built supercross track. It had been raining a lot in California and this track was one of the only areas that could absorb so much water. Jeremy struggled with his bike the entire time, though he was still fast enough to impress the onlookers.

After that, Jeremy went to Stefan Elvyn's private supercross track, and again things didn't feel right. With the AMA supercross kickoff just a few days away, the cruel reality of the situation was finally sitting in. Jeremy called an impromptu meeting with his family and explained what was going on inside his head and how his body had been affected. When the meeting ended, Jeremy decided he was done racing at that level. The following Monday, the McGraths made a list of friends and sponsors. They wanted to give everyone the news firsthand. When Jeremy's sister Tracy called

The seven-time AMA Supercross Champ was injured just a few weeks after this photo was shot. He dislocated his hip and was taken to Inland Valley Medical Center in nearby Wildomar, California, where he had to be knocked out so a team of doctors could put everything back into place. **Ken Faught/Dirt Rider**

me, I was completely blown away by the news, but I somehow knew he was making the right decision. Jeremy always told me that he would never race for second, and he was keeping his word even though it meant leaving several million dollars on the table.

"It was the most difficult decision of my life," Jeremy says. "I gave it everything I had, but it seemed like an uphill battle. It was the first time since I started

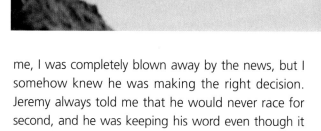

Bud Light stopped supporting McGrath immediately after he announced his retirement. Jeremy ran these graphics during a bike test for *Dirt Rider* magazine. **Ken Faught/Dirt Rider**

racing that I encountered so many problems in such a short time. All of these things were pretty strong indicators that it was time to get out."

Jeremy had never signed a KTM deal, although they had pretty much come to terms. He gave back $500,000 to Anheuser-Busch for his Bud Light sponsorship, and then renegotiated his deals with everyone from Works Connection to Parts Unlimited.

Jeremy was non-committal about his future. He owned his half-million-dollar semi-trailer, still had team personnel on the payroll, and really wanted to run his own team. In the end, Jeremy disbanded McGrath Racing and left many wondering what would have happened had he stayed with Yamaha. Had he ridden YZs, he wouldn't have been hurt testing fuel tanks, he wouldn't have been riding tentatively overseas, and he wouldn't have been knocked out. Instead, he might have fixed his arm pump problems of 2002 and entered Anaheim Stadium with a whole different outlook.

The Last-Minute Announcement Heard Around the World

The first round of the supercross series is always complicated by holidays and the New Year. While most companies shut down, those involved in the racing community are in full scramble mode trying to wrap up last-minute details. After all, the season opener is arguably the most important event of the year. It's the first time fans get to see riders on new bikes. The world gets to see who's hot and who's not, and a wide array of new products arrive on the scene.

The festivities include a press conference on Thursday with every major factory rider, team member, sponsor, photographer, and journalist in attendance. It's the who's who of supercross

It was a very emotional day for the McGrath family and the estimated 300 people inside the press box at Anaheim Stadium who witnessed Jeremy's retirement speech. **Scott Hoffman/ Dirt Rider**

"Throughout my whole career I've had something inside me that let's me know when I'm on and when I'm not. The day I got hurt was a bad day. I wasn't on that day. I had never been hurt that badly. I've always asked myself why guys have problems when they come back from injury. Now I know why. You start to think about everything you do out there because you don't want to get hurt again. Everything you do is supposed to be a natural reaction. You can do it blindfolded. Then if you start thinking about it and questioning yourself then it's time to step away.

"This was new to me because I've managed to stay free from serious injuries for most of my career. I put myself on the right position on the track and by calculating what was ahead of me I could stay out of harm's way. For the most part, I have been able to ride at a high speed without riding over my head. I think my limits were high but I never rode by the seat of my pants. That's just not my style.

"I think I'm getting out at the right time. I don't believe in racing past your prime. There was no way I was going to go out there and milk it. That would be unfair to everybody including myself. My legacy, the way I'll be remembered, is important to me. I've worked hard to get in the position I am now. When I was younger I watched Jeff Ward, who was a legend in my mind. I think he raced two or three seasons too long. Jeff had an unbelievable career, but I felt bad for him because it dragged on a bit too long. Ever since then, when I was a young kid, I thought I would never do that.

"What I want to be remembered for, aside from all the championships and victories, is that I was someone that the public could relate to. I never tried to be somebody that I wasn't. I always tried to be real and a good representative of the sport. That was something I got from my parents and it's always been important to me."

racing, though it's more a formality than a real news event. The 2003 press conference, however, was unusual. The McGraths had an announcement to make, and it would have an impact unlike any the sport had ever seen. Two hours before the normal press conference held by Clear Channel (the promoters of supercross), Jeremy slowly walked up to the table, sat down, and told the world that it was time to call it a career.

For many, the news hit hard. It meant the McGrath era was over and the sport was in search of a new superstar. Ricky Carmichael was well on his way to becoming the winningest rider in AMA history, but he wasn't accepted well by the fans. Travis Pastrana was struggling with injury and seemed too distracted with freestyle and extreme sports to be a real factor in stadium racing. With MC out, James Stewart would have to step up to the plate. His flashy riding style and charisma were important for the continued growth of supercross.

Attendance was down after word spread of Jeremy's exodus. The King of Supercross hit the road and went to all but two rounds to do a final lap aboard his works KTM 250SX. The year 2003 was truly a unique time in the sport's history and was billed as Jeremy's Farewell Tour. Huge lines formed around the Parts Unlimited ceremony where the seven-time champion signed more autographs than any other rider during the season. By the 16th round in Las Vegas, a decade of dominance officially came to an end.

Chapter Eight

MC's All About Fun

Long Beach Grand Prix, Hillclimbing, Supermoto, and More

Everyone expected McGrath to slip into retirement life immediately after announcing his intentions, and why wouldn't they? Jeff Stanton, Damon Bradshaw, Doug Henry, Jeff Emig, and a host of other superstars all but disappeared during the months that followed their exits. But McGrath is different. Although his body and once lightening-quick reflexes may not have been sharp enough for the 2003 supercross season, the champ still wanted to race and be competitive.

Jeremy McGrath—factory Toyota driver for a day. **Ken Faught/Dirt Rider**

"I always said that I never wanted to race for second," says McGrath. "Racing for me wasn't about the money. Of course the money was great, but I was out there for the challenge and the satisfaction of knowing that I was the best. I turned down several million dollars to race supercross, but that didn't mean I was done enjoying life."

In April 2003, McGrath signed on with the Long Beach Grand Prix Celebrity race in Southern California. This is a one-off race where actors, athletes, and other racers face off in identically prepared Toyota Celicas on the same streets where guys like Paul Tracy do 195 miles per hour in their Champ Cars.

McGrath managed to win the pro class and topped Buzz Aldrin (astronaut), Angie Everhart (actress), Jesse James (owner of West Coast Choppers), Picabo Street (Olympic skier), Adam Carolla (actor), Tony Potts (Access Hollywood), and a half-dozen other drivers. McGrath spent several days preparing for the charity race by taking a Toyota-sponsored driving course at Willow Springs Raceway in nearby Rosamond, California.

"The whole experience was incredible," McGrath said on the day of the event. "I love a new challenge, and I really enjoy learning."

McGrath also spends a lot of his time at the river with his speed boat and playing around on Honda XR50s. McGrath even built his own 50 track where he and his friends can bang bars on their ultra-pricey custom mini bikes. He has also gotten into supermoto racing (more on that later).

Jeremy got the hillclimbing bug after watching me do it two years earlier on Speedvision (which is now called Speed Channel). Jeremy and I were with Trevor Vines at Yamaha's 2001 team introduction when Jeremy asked me what it was like. I explained it to him, and the little-known extreme sport piqued his curiosity. I told him that I could get bikes for him to ride if he ever wanted to give it a shot. In 2003, he took me up on the offer.

I called Kerry Peterson, the most celebrated hill-climb rider of the modern era. Although he's retired,

> "I've always respected the way Jeremy carried himself. He's an amazing person on and off the track, and I'm glad that he's working with us today. He's an inspiration to people all over the world, and I don't think there's anyone out there who didn't enjoy watching his amazing career."
>
> —Jeff Fox, Parts Unlimited

Jeremy McGrath's first attempt at professional hillclimbing earned him a spot in history books. Aboard this Honda CR500R, he finished second overall in the Montana State Championship at the most prestigious event in America. **Ken Faught/Dirt Rider** the five-time world champion is still very much involved with his two sons, Robie and Brett. The trio has a giant fleet of bikes that includes everything from extended swingarm Honda CR500s to nitro-injected Harley-Davidsons. They even have a 700cc two-stroke built by a company called Zabel that specializes in sidecar engines. If that's not exotic enough, they have a normally aspirated 2500cc Harley that pumps out 218 horsepower and a twin-engine Honda that uses a pair of CR500 motors.

Class rules normally do not allow bike sharing among riders. The Billings Motorcycle Club allowed Jeremy to share bikes with Robie in two classes, but made it clear that Jeremy was not

Jeremy McGrath next to his borrowed 218-horsepower Harley-Davidson. "This bike actually scared me when they first started it up," said McGrath. "It got even scarier once I let the clutch out." Still, McGrath took this thing over the top. **Ken Faught/Dirt Rider**

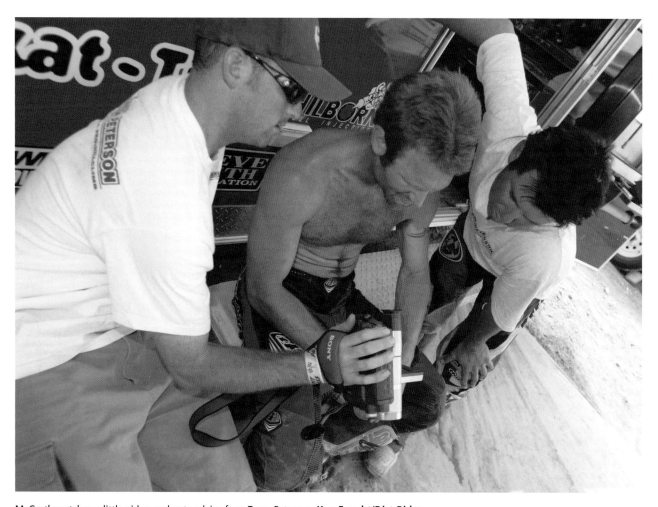

McGrath watches a little video and gets advice from Team Peterson. **Ken Faught/Dirt Rider**

Kerry and Debbie Peterson will always have this signed jersey to remember Billings 2003. **Ken Faught/Dirt Rider**

eligible for prize money or championship points. In the 0–600cc and the 0–700cc classes, MC alone rode Team Peterson's Honda CR500.

When Jeremy and I arrived in Montana, I used the same trick Karel Kramer used on me a few years earlier. I drove our rental car the back way to the top of the hill and had him look at it from that vantage point. Jeremy looked me straight into the eyes and said, "What have you gotten me into?"

A few weeks earlier, Jeremy had spent two hours at my house watching hillclimbing videos. He knew it was one of the sports that looked easier on television than it was in reality, and now he got his first glimpse of the real difficulty.

After 15 minutes on top, we hopped into the rental car and hooked up with the Peterson family in the pits. After the introductions, we suited up, and went out in the nearby hills to get used to the bikes.

Aside from the slow turning personality, the most difficult thing to get used to is the fact that these bikes don't have rear brakes. Because the riders change the swingarm length routinely to adjust for changing hills in their quest for more or less traction, they don't have time to bleed disc brakes.

"That was probably the scariest thing for me," says Jeremy. "When we were playing around on Friday with Robie and Brett, I came down this one hill and forgot I only had the front brake. I was hauling and saw a big g-out at the bottom, and hit that sucker going way too fast. That was the first and the last time I forgot about the brake situation."

Jeremy's debut at Billings was impressive by all accounts—he finished fifth in one class and ninth in another. His fifth in the 0–600cc class qualified him for a spot in the 12-rider Montana State Shootout. The promoters open up the entire hill, normally filled with course-marking flags, and give them a straight shot up the 420-foot incline. Jeremy and Travis Whitlock put on a riding clinic, and even started doubling over a ledge at the base of the championship hill. In the shootout, McGrath finished second behind Whitlock and made it over the top five out of nine times.

"I had so much fun this weekend," said McGrath. "This is one of the strangest things I've ever done, but it was an incredible experience. I'm really impressed the way some of these guys ride. It takes a lot of guts, but it also takes a lot of talent."

"Jeremy impressed everyone here," said Whitlock. "Jeremy rode well all weekend long, and I think he would have done better, but he started celebrating too early a couple times. There are timing lights 50 feet down the backside of the hill, and a couple times he started pumping his fist in the air."

"I blew it," said Jeremy. "I knew the lights were there, but I forgot. I guess I just got caught up in the moment."

"McGrath is a racer's racer," said Kerry Peterson. "He's just a class act. I have so much respect for him as an athlete and a person, and I hope he comes back. He certainly made this event fun, and he didn't do it for the money. Jeremy turned out to be a huge fan of hill-climbing, and what made this even more remarkable was the fact that he never saw his race bikes before he

Robie Peterson, the oldest of the Peterson sons, rode injured throughout most of the weekend. **Ken Faught/Dirt Rider**

arrived in Montana. He only had an hour to practice, and never rode the 2500cc Harley before his run. Even on the 'big iron' he got up, and I've never seen anyone do that on an unfamiliar bike. I really think he's the best all-around motorcycle rider that has ever lived!"

Supermoto

A few months after retiring from AMA Supercross, there was a new attraction in the two-wheel world for Jeremy. Long-time friend and famed helmet painter Troy Lee talked him into a day of supermoto riding aboard a modified Honda CRF450R. The hybrid sport of racing dirt bikes on pavement has been popular in Europe for more than a decade. It also has a place in American history thanks to an annual broadcast during the 1980s of an event at the Carlsbad Raceway called SuperBikers. The race appeared on ABC's Wide World of Sports and was one of the rare occasions when off-road motorcycling was on television. In those days, satellite and cable television was rare, and motorcycle programming was virtually non-existent.

McGrath loved dragging his knees on asphalt, sliding both tires under hard braking, and battling with heroes from other aspects of the motorcycle world. It renewed his enthusiasm while he was still recovering from the dislocated hip sustained a few months earlier.

About the same time, the supermoto phenomenon started to take off in a big way. Guys from the road racing world like Kevin Schwantz, Scott Russell, and Jake Zempke started facing off against motocrossers like Jeff Ward and Kurt Nicole and freestylers like Mike Metzger. Then a bunch of small series events started to pop up all over the United States, and that's when Troy

Cameras followed McGrath everywhere he went in Montana, and every major television station in Billings sent out a crew to document his runs. **Ken Faught/Dirt Rider**

Team Peterson 2004 also included former Grand National Cross Country champ Shane Watts and *Dirt Rider* magazine's Karel Kramer and Ken Faught. **Mark Baltadono**

Lee decided to create his own team. He talked to McGrath and Ward, and then approached Honda with the idea of supporting this unique trio in the new effort. It was the first time since 1996 that McGrath had anything to do with the Big Red team.

Lee worked out a deal with Giant RV and Fleetwood to score a $220,000 Revolution quad-slide motor home. He also worked out a deal to get a massive trailer big enough to put them 2 feet over the legal limit in the state of California. It created a lot of headaches for driver Scott Bell (brother of 1980 AMA Supercross Champion Mike Bell), but anyone who knows Troy comes to expect things like this.

During the first round of the AMA Red Bull Supermoto Series at Laguna Seca Raceway in north-

McGrath, Brett Peterson, and friends await the awards ceremony. **Ken Faught/Dirt Rider**

ern California, Troy crashed hard. Because the series was a three-rider team format, Troy hired Jake Zempke as a replacement rider. The team also recruited Chad Watts to wrench for the factory-supported effort. If the name sounds familiar, it's because Watts was Ricky Carmichael's mechanic up to that point. He and RC had a well-publicized falling out midway through the 2003 season, and Watts had just left Honda to start a company called Watts Perfections based in Corona, California. It was an ideal situation for Team Troy Lee Designs, since its shop is located only 2 miles away from the performance giant.

Jeff Ward proved to be the dominant rider in the series. It was fitting since he was one of Jeremy's favorite riders growing up. Jeremy even had posters of Wardy on his bedroom wall. Ward left a successful motocross and supercross career with Kawasaki to head into the world of open-wheel racing. He did well at events like the Indianapolis 500 where speeds reach in excess of 230 miles per hour. Ward combined both skills and came up just a hair faster than Jeremy most of the time.

Even though their dad beat Jeremy in the state shootout, Travis Whitlock's girls couldn't resist an autograph from King MC. **Ken Faught/Dirt Rider**

Shannon Chamberlain and Jeremy McGrath flank Travis Whitlock in the winner's circle. **Ken Faught/Dirt Rider**

"I look at McGrath as being similar to one of several athletes that took their respective action sport to new heights during recent times. Lance Armstrong in cycling, Tony Hawk in skateboarding, Mat Hoffman in freestyle BMX, Shaun Palmer in snowboarding, Phil and Steve Mahre in skiing, Carl Lewis in track and field are several names synonymous with elevating a non-mainstream sport to national attention levels."

**—Pat Schutte, OMS Sports,
former PR Manager for Supercross**

"I really have a lot of fun racing with Troy and Jeff," says Jeremy. "This sport is so much fun. It doesn't have a lot of pressure, and I can relax and be myself. I hope supermoto will be around a long time."

"Most of the tracks are 70 percent asphalt, 30 percent dirt," McGrath says. "The jumps are really small and the turns are flat. The racing resembles road racing and dirt track more than motocross, but that doesn't really hurt me. The courses are so unique that it doesn't really favor riders from one particular form of motorcycle racing."

From a technical standpoint, supermoto race bikes begin life as normal motocross bikes. Most riders prefer 450cc four-strokes because of the smooth power, precise handling, and lightweight feel. Mechanics remove the 21-inch front and 18-inch rear wheels, and throw on a set of 17s. The new wheels are fitted with extra-wide road racing tires that are generally slicks, although at some tracks the riders cut "grooves" in them manually to enhance performance. The suspension is also dropped a few inches to lower the center of gravity. Riders don't need 12 inches of travel, since the few jumps that are on the course aren't that big. There might be a 4-foot-high tabletop and a few whoops, but nothing more extreme.

Things start to get a little tricky with engines because most modifications severely hinder endurance. Riders generally bump up compression and run a complete aftermarket exhaust. So far, factory involvement hasn't hurt the sport in this low-budget form of racing. Talent still outweighs a thick wallet, but that will probably change as the sport gets more media attention.

Riders also run an oversized front rotor, a steel brake line, and a street-bike-style master cylinder. Stopping power, traction, and horsepower are king in this sport, and that produces some radical setups.

"We're still learning a lot about bike setup," says McGrath. "There's so much to try out there, and the possibilities are endless. Since the sport is so new, everybody is at the same disadvantage. And when someone *does* come up with something that works, no one likes to talk about it. There's a lot of secrets out there, and that makes testing extremely important. We have a lot of talented people working on our team, and so far, we've had real competitive equipment."

McGrath's 2500cc Harley required a starter to get the beast lit. **Ken Faught/Dirt Rider**

McGrath and the author, Ken Faught, study lines with Mel Kimball.
Karel Kramer/Dirt Rider

Jeremy helps hillclimbing legend Kerry Peterson rebuild the Harley clutch in between runs. **Ken Faught/Dirt Rider**

"The Harley was so fast that I don't think I ever let the clutch all the way out," said McGrath. "Even in the burnout area I was afraid that I might loop it out." **Ken Faught/ Dirt Rider**

"One of the neatest things about this sport is that you can make a track almost anywhere," says Troy Lee. "In most cases, we run on go-cart tracks or on modified road race courses in conjunction with the AMA Superbike series. We've even raced in a couple parking lots, plus we've ridden on the streets of downtown Long Beach, California. It really amazes me how much fun it is, and how quickly it's growing. It also doesn't hurt that it has a lot of really recognizable names during the first year, and we're all glad to see that MC seems to be having the time of his life."

In the middle of October 2003, McGrath surprised a lot of people by packing his bags and heading overseas. He flew to England and won a small supercross aboard a Honda CR250R. It was the first time since 1996 that MC raced a Honda two-stroke.

With Jeremy still showing strong interest in racing two wheels, there were all sorts of rumors about a comeback. In fact, at the end of 2003, Kawasaki called and offered him a deal to be teammates with Michael Byrne.

"Jeremy thought about it for 24 hours and then told them no," says Kim McGrath. "What's funny is that people started hearing about it a few weeks later and then all sorts of rumors were on the internet. Everyone kept asking him about the Kawasaki deal, and no matter what he said, people still thought he was taking the offer."

"I don't know what I want to do," McGrath said during the 2004 Supercross season finale in Las Vegas. "For a while, I never thought I would ever race a supercross again, but after sitting out two seasons, I kind of miss it. I'm exploring a lot of my options right now and might come back and race supercross for a season or two. I feel refreshed, I'm completely healthy, and if I have the right bike, who knows what could happen. If not, I've had an incredible career, and I have no regrets."

Without McGrath, supercross wouldn't have had the head start that it did on the rest of the action sports community. Supercross would have *become* popular based on the action sports movement and athletes like Travis Pastrana, Ricky Carmichael, Mike LaRocco, and James Stewart. But McGrath launched the sport of supercross into the extreme/action sport stratosphere several years *before* the "X Games" craze came to fruition. The advantage was that supercross was able to lay claim to being the "Reigning King of Extreme Sports" based almost solely on the name "McGrath."

Top: "It looks a lot easier on television," said McGrath. **Ken Faught/Dirt Rider**

Right: McGrath charges up the hill on a CR500R with its wheelbase extended over a foot to 66 inches. **Ken Faught/ Dirt Rider**

"Jeremy McGrath has impacted the sport a lot more than even his incredible record of 7 supercross championships and 72 AMA supercross wins. McGrath has set new and higher standards for just about every measure of success in the sport; he even found his limits as far as what all his fame and winning can lead to, too.

"Other champions and front-runners look to McGrath as a role model in many ways. McGrath was supercross' first rock star. His warm personality and humble demeanor won over fans, media, and industry types. Now if you want to talk about how popular a supercross champion should be or how popular he can be, you have to think about McGrath. He is the standard. When you want to talk about how popular Ricky Carmichael is at this point in his career, you can hardly do it without comparing him to McGrath at the same time.

"If you think just about speed and skill on the track, McGrath set a standard there, too. He brought technical skill with him from BMX racing, used this to figure out how to ride supercross faster than everyone else was going in 1993, and he did it consistently.

"McGrath was very fast and very smooth, and just as importantly, he respected his bike and only rode to his limits. Injuries for him were rare. If someone else was a little faster on a certain night, he would still stick to his own safest speed instead of throwing away a race taking chances. That's a standard other top riders look at too, like a 'safe supercross speed limit.' To go faster than McGrath did, you have to ride a little on the edge, as Ricky Carmichael did in 2001 to win the championship for himself.

"McGrath even changed how writers think about a supercross race. For almost a decade, every supercross story was a story on McGrath. If he won, we expected that. Life is normal. If McGrath didn't win, we wanted to know why. He was that good.

"Finally, McGrath set standards for what doesn't work as well. Other top riders thinking about life outside the factory umbrella all look to McGrath's experiences. The blowout with Honda led to rushing into a spot with Suzuki in 1997, and this didn't work. The deal with Bud Light seemed like it could lead to a significant new era for supercross where a big outside sponsor eclipses what the factory teams are doing, but problems with finding teammates that met the beer company's guidelines (McGrath needed to hire top 250 riders that were over 25 and not locked into a factory deal) stalled the growth. Then when McGrath decided not to race in 2003, the deal evaporated. Anyone in Carmichael's camp that wants to spin off a 'Carmichael Racing' and try the same thing would look at McGrath's experience for a reality check.

"So it doesn't matter if you are talking about skill, race results, popularity, or longevity in supercross, everything comes back to what happened to McGrath. That's a legacy that is unlikely to ever fade."

—Steve Bruhn, Owner/founder of motonews.com

I worked with McGrath for two years, when he won his title back from Jeff Emig in 1998 and when he defended it in 1999. It was amazing to see how dominant the guy was during that time. I remember being in the press box and already having my race story written—and the qualifiers were just starting! During that two-year span, arguably when McGrath was at his best, McGrath won 14 races, including five straight in 1999. I'd ask other riders, "What's up with this guy? How come he's so dominant?"

McGrath was, without a doubt, inside everybody's head during his seven supercross championships and maybe never-to-be-touched 72 supercross wins.

Jeremy's mom, Ann, and wife, Kim, are two of his biggest supporters. **Ken Faught/Dirt Rider**

All of the cars were identically prepped for the celebrity and pro challenge drivers. They even spent several days at a nearby driving school in Southern California to get tips from the pros. **Ken Faught/Dirt Rider**

Actress Angie Everhart was one of the many celebrity drivers who attracted a lot of media attention. **Ken Faught/Dirt Rider**

It's been a long time since MC's worn an open face helmet in his racing career, but it's probably not going to be the last. Rumor has it that McGrath plans on racing in a few more car races in the coming years. **Ken Faught/Dirt Rider**

The champ cars reach speeds up to 190 miles per hour on the temporary road course that runs down the city streets of Long Beach, California. **Ken Faught/Dirt Rider**

Olympic skier Picabo Street and Jeremy were interviewed by Dave Stanfield for ESPN shortly before qualifying. **Ken Faught/Dirt Rider**

McGrath chases television personality Steve Hartman and famed custom street bike builder Jesse James down one of the fastest sections of the course. **Ken Faught/Dirt Rider**

Actress and model Angie Everhart kisses astronaut Buzz Aldrin as the rest of the celebrity and pro drivers mess around for the token group shot. **Ken Faught/Dirt Rider**

Jeremy McGrath tried his hand at supermoto at the end of 2002 and then made a full assault on the 2003 series. It comes as no surprise that the supercross hole shot master starts many races at the head of the pack. **Ken Faught/ Dirt Rider**

Supermoto bikes don't get much more high-tech than MC's Pro Circuit-built Honda CRF450R. In addition to lowered suspension and a massive oversize front rotor, he runs pure slicks at most events. **Ken Faught/Dirt Rider**

"I think the one thing that makes McGrath stand out as the greatest came in the summer of 1995 when he won the 250cc Outdoor National title. Had he not done that, critics would have pointed to him as being 'the best supercross racer ever.' But I believe his National title cements his status as the greatest ever. Period."

—Pat Schutte, OMS Sports

One appealing aspect of supermoto is that courses can be set up almost anywhere, such as this resort parking lot in the Rocky Mountains. **Ken Faught/Dirt Rider**

Line choice is really critical, especially at the start when the pack is bunched up. McGrath and gang regularly reach speeds over 100 miles per hour on the asphalt, where mistakes can be painful. **Ken Faught/Dirt Rider**

Former AMA champ Jeff Ward was on McGrath's team for 2003, along with road racer Jake Zempke and famed helmet painter Troy Lee. Ward was one of the fastest and most consistent riders during the inaugural series. **Ken Faught/Dirt Rider**

Traction is incredible with Dunlop slicks. The big Honda four-stroke accelerates hard off asphalt corners with very little wheelspin. **Ken Faught/Dirt Rider**

Kevin Schwantz, the 1993 500cc Road Race World Champion, is one of the many top riders who come from other motorcycle racing extremes. The Yoshimura Suzuki rider won this non-series event in Copper Mountain, Colorado, as part of the first Colorado Cyclefest. **Ken Faught/Dirt Rider**

Supermoto requires totally different techniques than those used in motocross or supercross. Here McGrath backs it into this 180-degree right-hand turn. **Ken Faught/Dirt Rider**

"In the end, what I'll probably remember most about McGrath was this one time (of many) when he had a 'Make-A-Wish' Foundation kid in tow. We were hanging out in the Chaparral truck and McGrath turned to me and said, 'You know, sometimes I think that this Make-A-Wish stuff is more for the parents than the kid,' watching the father of the Make-A-Wish child scrambling to get as much McGrath swag from Randy Lawrence and Larry Brooks as he could. McGrath reflected for a moment, then said, 'Yeah, but still, I think that's OK.'

"Wherever he goes these days, from supermoto races to events in the auto industry, McGrath continues to be the premier ambassador of the sport. And though he's passed the supercross title torch on to Carmichael and Chad Reed, hopefully he'll boot up and race a supercross here and there. Podium or not, his presence would certainly be beneficial for the sport!"

—PAT SCHUTTE, OMS SPORTS

Dirt-track-style corners are challenging with slick tires, but McGrath has always been known for his incredible throttle control, body positioning, and quick reflexes. **Ken Faught/Dirt Rider**

Notice the huge front brake master cylinder on the right side of the handlebar. Supermoto bikes have incredible stopping power. **Ken Faught/Dirt Rider**

On most supermoto courses, there are very few jumps, and they can be tricky with lowered suspension, but that's where Jeremy continues to feel most comfortable. **Ken Faught/Dirt Rider**

Appendix A
Records and Cool Facts

McGRATH'S WIN LIST

7-time AMA 250cc Supercross Champion (1993–1996, 1998–2000)
2-time AMA 125cc Western Region SX Champion (1991–1992)
1-time AMA 250cc National MX Champion (1995)
72 – AMA 250cc Supercross wins
13 – AMA 125cc Western Region SX wins
2 – AMA 125cc National Championship wins
15 – AMA 250cc National Championship wins

McGRATH'S MAIN RIVALS

1993 – Jeff Stanton and Mike Kiedrowski
1994 – Mike LaRocco and Mike Kiedrowski
1995 – Mike LaRocco
1996 – No one!
1997 – Jeff Emig and the slipping Suzuki clutch
1998 – Jeff Emig and Ezra Lusk
1999 – Ezra Lusk
2000 – Ricky Carmichael and David Vuillemin
2001 – Every factory rider, and top privateers
2002 – Arm pump

INTERESTING FACTS

-McGrath is the youngest rider inducted into the AMA Motorcycle Hall of Fame (October 2003)

-McGrath never missed starting a 250cc Supercross between 1993 and 2002

-2002 was the first time in his career that he didn't win at least one race

-McGrath never won a 125cc East/West SX Shootout

-Going into the 2003 season, McGrath was still the world's most popular rider

-McGrath owns Clutch Films (producers of the Steel Roots series) with best friend Lawrence Lewis

-Jeremy raced for all five major manufacturers as a pro

-Skip Norfolk was with McGrath throughout his professional career (except for a short stint when Randy Lawrence and Wyatt Seals spun wrenches for MC)

-Only AMA numbers: 125, 15, 3, 2, 1

-Jeremy worked at a Vons grocery store for five months bagging groceries

-MC's second job was at Raceway Honda in Perris, California

-As a kid, Jeremy did clean-up work around his parents' muffler shop

-Jeremy appeared on *The Tonight Show* with Jay Leno twice

-Kim Erin Maddox became Mrs. McGrath on August 3, 2002, in Orange County, California

-Jeremy had a cameo in Disney's hit movie *Motocrossed*

-Jeremy made a cameo appearance in *Charlie's Angels* with Cameron Diaz, Lucy Liu, and Drew Barrymore

OTHER WINS and CHAMPIONSHIPS

-1992 World Supercross Champion

-1995 World Supercross Champion

-Motocross des Nations in 1996 in Jerez, Spain, with teammates Steve Lamson and Jeff Emig

The Motocross des Nations win in Jerez, Spain at the end of the 1996 season was one of the highlights of McGrath's outdoor career. Ken Faught/Dirt Rider

AMA 125cc WESTERN REGION SUPERCROSS RACE RESULTS

1990 - Anaheim, CA	1
1990 - Houston, TX*	21
1990 - San Diego, CA	2
1990 - Seattle, WA	2
1990 - Las Vegas, NV	1
1990 - Pasadena, CA	3
1990 - Dallas, TX*	3
1990 - Oklahoma City, OK*	2
1990 - San Jose, CA	6
1990 - Los Angeles, CA	3
1990 Series Position	2

Served as an East/West round

1991 - Houston, TX*	2
1991 - Anaheim, CA	1
1991 - Seattle, WA	1
1991 - San Diego, CA	1
1991 - Phoenix, AZ	3
1991 - Dallas, TX	1
1991 - Las Vegas, NV	1
1991 – Oklahoma City, OK	2
1991 - San Jose, CA	9
1991 - Los Angeles, CA	0
1991 Series Position	1

Served as an East/West round

1992 - Houston, TX	3*
1992 - Anaheim, CA	1
1992 - Seattle, WA	1
1992 - San Diego, CA	1
1992 - Las Vegas, NV	1
1992 - Dallas, TX	1*
1992 - San Jose, CA	1
1992 - Los Angeles, CA	1
1992 Series Position	1

Combined East/West Region event

AMA 250cc SUPERCROSS RACE RESULTS

1992 - Orlando, FL	Did Not Start (DNS)
1992 - Atlanta, GA	DNS
1992 - Daytona Beach, FL	20
1992 - Charlotte, NC	10
1992 - Indianapolis, IN	6
1992 - Tampa, FL	5
1992 - Pontiac, MI	8
1992 - Pontiac, MI	6
1992 Series Position	16*

Rode 125 Western Region at the other events on the schedule

1993 - Orlando, FL	4
1993 - Houston, TX	5
1993 - Anaheim, CA	1
1993 - Seattle, WA	1
1993 - San Diego, CA	1
1993 - Tampa, FL	1
1993 - Atlanta, GA	4
1993 - Daytona Beach, FL	2
1993 - Dallas, TX	1
1993 - Charlotte, NC	1
1993 - Pontiac, MI	1
1993 - Indianapolis, IN	1
1993 - Pasadena, CA	1
1993 - San Jose, CA	1
1993 - Las Vegas, NV	9
1993 Series Position	1

1994 - Orlando, FL	1
1994 - Houston, TX	1
1994 - Anaheim, CA	1
1994 - San Diego, CA	1
1994 - Tampa, FL	1
1994 - Atlanta, GA	1
1994 - Daytona Beach, FL	4
1994 - Indianapolis, IN	1

1994 - Charlotte, NC	7
1994 - Pontiac, MI	1
1994 - Minneapolis, MN	1
1994 - Dallas, TX	3
1994 - Seattle, WA	3
1994 - San Jose, CA	2
1994 - Las Vegas, NV	1
1994 Series Position	1
1995 - Orlando, FL	1
1995 - Minneapolis, MN	1
1995 - Anaheim, CA	1
1995 - Seattle, WA	1
1995 - San Diego, CA	1
1995 - Atlanta, GA	4
1995 - Daytona Beach, FL	7
1995 - Indianapolis, IN	1
1995 - Houston, TX	1
1995 - Pontiac, MI	5
1995 - Charlotte, NC	1
1995 - Dallas, TX	2
1995 - Cleveland, OH	1
1995 - San Jose, CA	1
1995 - Las Vegas, CA	DNS*
1995 Series Position	1

(due to city power failure)

1996 - Orlando, FL	1
1996 - Minneapolis, MN	1
1996 - Anaheim, CA	1
1996 - Seattle, WA	1
1996 - San Diego, CA	1
1996 - Atlanta, GA	1
1996 - Daytona Beach, FL	1
1996 - Houston, TX	1
1996 - Dallas, TX	1
1996 - Indianapolis, IN	1
1996 - Tampa, FL	1

1996 - Pontiac, MI	1
1996 - Charlotte, NC	1
1996 - St. Louis, MO	2
1996 - Denver, CO	1
1996 Series Position	1
1997 - Los Angeles, CA	15
1997 - Los Angeles, CA	3
1997 - Tempe, AZ	2
1997 - Seattle, WA	2
1997 - Indianapolis, IN	9
1997 - Atlanta, GA	3
1997 - Daytona Beach, FL	3
1997 - Minneapolis, MN	1
1997 - Houston, TX	3
1997 - Orlando, FL	2
1997 - St. Louis, MO	1
1997 - Pontiac, MI	4
1997 - Charlotte, NC	7
1997 - Dallas, TX	4
1997 - Las Vegas, NV	7
1997 Series Position	2

Jeremy was all business in 1997, shown here on the phone at Guy Cooper's shop in Stillwater, Oklahoma.
Ken Faught/Dirt Rider

1998 - Los Angeles, CA	1
1998 - Houston, TX	2
1998 - Tempe, AZ	2
1998 - Seattle, WA	1
1998 - San Diego, CA	1
1998 - Indianapolis, IN	1
1998 - Atlanta, GA	1
1998 - Tampa, FL	8
1998 - Daytona Beach, FL	1
1998 - New Orleans, LA	2
1998 - Minneapolis, MN	1
1998 - St. Louis, MO	4
1998 - Pontiac, MI	20
1998 - Charlotte, NC	14
1998 - Dallas, TX	2
1998 - Las Vegas, NV	1
1998 Series Position	1
1999 - Anaheim, CA	7
1999 - San Diego, CA	2
1999 - Phoenix, AZ	1
1999 - Seattle, WA	4
1999 - Anaheim, CA	2
1999 - Tampa, FL	2
1999 - Atlanta, GA	1
1999 - Dallas, TX	4
1999 - Daytona Beach, FL	1
1999 - Houston, TX	1
1999 - Minneapolis, MN	1
1999 - St. Louis, MO	1
1999 - Pontiac, MI	1
1999 - New Orleans, LA	2
1999 - Indianapolis, IN	4
1999 - Las Vegas, NV	1
1999 Series Position	1
2000 - Anaheim, CA	1
2000 - Anaheim, CA	1

2000 - San Diego, CA	4
2000 - Phoenix, AZ	2
2000 - Houston, TX	1
2000 - Indianapolis, IN	1
2000 - Pontiac, MI	1
2000 - Atlanta, GA	1
2000 - Daytona Beach, FL	2
2000 - St. Louis, MO	1
2000 - Minneapolis, MN	3
2000 - Pontiac, MI	1
2000 - Dallas, TX	4
2000 - New Orleans, LA	2
2000 - Joliet, IL	1
2000 - Las Vegas, NV	1
2000 Series Position	1
2001 - Anaheim, CA	1
2001 - San Diego, CA	3
2001 - Anaheim, CA	1
2001 - Phoenix, AZ	2
2001 - Anaheim, CA	2
2001 - Indianapolis, IN	2
2001 - Atlanta, GA	2
2001 - New Orleans, LA	4
2001 - Daytona Beach, CA	6
2001 - Minneapolis, MN	2
2001 - Houston, TX	2
2001 - St. Louis, MO	4
2001 - Pontiac, MI	4
2001 - Dallas, TX	3
2001 - Salt Lake City, UT	6
2001 - Las Vegas, NV	2
2001 Series Position	2
2002 - Anaheim, CA	13
2002 - San Diego, CA	10
2002 - Anaheim, CA	9
2002 - Phoenix, AZ	6

AMA 250cc SUPERCROSS RACE RESULTS (continued)

2002 - Anaheim, CA	6
2002 - Indianapolis, IN	7
2002 - Minneapolis, MN	6
2002 - Atlanta, GA	3
2002 - Daytona Beach, FL	5
2002 - New Orleans, LA	4
2002 - Houston, TX	5
2002 - St. Louis, MO	4
2002 - Pontiac, MI	3
2002 - Dallas, TX	3
2002 - Salt Lake City, UT	5
2002 - Las Vegas, NV	5
2002 Series Position	3

AMA 125cc NATIONAL MX RACE RESULTS

1991 - Gainesville, FL	7
1991 - Prairie City, CA	10
1991 - Mt. Morris, PA	9
1991 - Buchanan, MI	7
1991 - Axton, VA	6
1991 - Troy, OH	7
1991 - Southwick, MA	5
1991 - Millville, MN	6
1991 - Washougal, WA	5
1991 - Binghamton, NY	6
1991 - Delmont, PA	5
1991 - Budds Creek, MD	5
1991 - New Berlin, NY	10
1991 Series Position	5
1992 - Gainesville, FL	5
1992 - Southwick, MA	4
1992 - Mt. Morris, PA	5
1992 - Prairie City, CA	8
1992 - Buchanan, MI	8
1992 - Troy, OH	22
1992 - Washougal, WA	5
1992 - Millville, MN	6
1992 - Binghamton, NY	13
1992 - Delmont, PA	15
1992 - Budds Creek, MD	9
1992 Series Position	8
1993 - Gainesville, FL	1
1993 - Southwick, MA	13
1993 - Mt. Morris, PA	3
1993 - Hangtown, CA	1
1993 - Red Bud, MI	2
1993 - Unidilla, NY	2
1993 - Troy, NY	4
1993 - Glen Helen, CA	8
1993 - Washougal, WA	3
1993 - Millville, MN	3
1993 - Delmont (Steel City), PA	5
1993 Series Position	5

1994 - Gainesville, FL	6	1996 - New Berlin, NY	2
1994 - Prairie City, CA	DNS	1996 - Troy, OH	1
1994 - Budds Creek, MD	2	1996 - Millville, MN	6
1994 - Mt. Morris, PA	3	1996 - Washougal, WA	15
1994 - Southwick, MA	4	1996 - Binghamton, NY	1
1994 - Buchanan, MI	12	1996 - Delmont, PA	2
1994 - New Berlin, NY	8	1996 Series position	2
1994 - Troy, OH	2		
1994 - Millville, MN	3	1997 - Gainesville, FL	2
1994 - Washougal, WA	2	1997 - Sacramento, CA	5
1994 - Binghamton, NY	6	1997 - San Bernardino, CA	4
1994 - Delmont, PA	2	1997 - Mt. Morris, PA	7
1994 Series Position	3	1997 - Budds Creek, MD	3
		1997 - Southwick, MA	5
1995 - Gainesville, FL	1	1997 - Buchanan, MI	3
1995 - Prairie City, CA	6	1997 - Unadilla, NY	8
1995 - Mt. Morris, PA	3	1997 - Troy, OH	3
1995 - Budds Creek, MD	1	1997 - Millville, MN	8
1995 - Southwick, MA	2	1997 - Washougal, WA	3
1995 - Buchanan, MI	1	1997 - Binghamton, NY	5
1995 - Troy, OH	1	1997 - Delmont, PA	6
1995 - New Berlin, NY	1	1997 Series position	3
1995 - Millville, MN	2		
1995 - Washougal, WA	1	1998 - San Bernardino, CA	2
1995 - Binghamton, NY	1	1998 - Prairie City, CA	1
1995 - Delmont, PA	1	1998 - Mt. Morris, PA	6
1995 Series Position	1	1998 - Southwick, MA	DNS
		1998 Series Position	14
1996 - Gainesville, FL	1		
1996 - Prairie City, CA	1	1999 - San Bernardino, CA	10
1996 - San Bernardino, CA	1	1999 Series Position	21
1996 - Mt. Morris, PA	3		
1996 - Budds Creek, MD	1		
1996 - Southwick, MA	1		
1996 - Buchanan, MI	1		

McGrath only raced two outdoor events in 1999. He created a supercross-only contract for himself because he felt his career would last longer by focusing on his indoor specialty.

1.	Jeremy McGrath	13	21.	Tyson Vohland	4
2.	Ricky Carmichael	12	21.	David Vuillemin	4
2.	Ernesto Fonseca	12	33.	Buddy Antunez	3
2.	Damon Huffman	12	33.	Larry Brooks	3
2.	Brian Swink	12	33.	Jeromy Buehl	3
2.	Kevin Windham	12	33.	Ty Davis	3
7.	Jeff Matiasevich	11	33.	Todd DeHoop	3
7.	James Stewart, Jr.	11	33.	Mike LaRocco	3
9.	Mickael Pichon	10	33.	Kyle Lewis	3
10.	Nathan Ramsey	9	33.	Eddie Warren	3
11.	Denny Stephenson	8	41.	Tyler Evans	2
11.	Keith Turpin	8	41.	Mike Healey	2
13.	John Dowd	7	41.	Casey Johnson	2
13.	Doug Henry	7	41.	Mike Kiedrowski	2
13.	Ezra Lusk	7	45.	Michael Brandes	1
13.	Travis Pastrana	7	46.	Justin Buckelew	1
13.	Stephane Roncada	7	46.	Todd Campbell	1
18.	Damon Bradshaw	6	46.	Mike Craig	1
18.	Jeff Emig	6	46.	Brian Deegan	1
18.	Chad Reed	6	46.	Jimmy Gaddis	1
21.	Mike Brown	4	46.	Pedro Gonzalez	1
21.	Jimmy Button	4	46.	Grant Langston	1
21.	Ryan Hughes	4	46.	Phil Lawrence	1
21.	Branden Jesseman	4	46.	Bader Manneh	1
21.	David Pingree	4	46.	Bobby Moore	1
21.	Travis Preston	4	46.	Chad Pederson	1
21.	Donnie Schmit	4	46.	Andrew Short	1
21.	Brock Sellards	4	46.	Ivan Tedesco	1
21.	Willie Surratt	4	46.	Matt Walker	1
21.	Ron Tichenor	4	46.	Jeff Willoh	1

1. Jeremy McGrath	72	24. Doug Henry	4
2. Ricky Carmichael	33	24. Jim Weinert	4
3. Rick Johnson	28	24. Darrell Shultz	4
4. Bob Hannah	27	24. Donnie Hansen	4
5. Jeff Ward	20	28. Marty Smith	3
6. Damon Bradshaw	19	28. Larry Ward	3
7. Mark Barnett	17	30. Tony DiStefano	2
7. Jeff Stanton	17	30. Marty Tripes	2
9. Jean-Michel Bayle	16	32. Damon Huffman	1
10. David Bailey	12	32. John Dowd	1
10. Ezra Lusk	12	32. Gaylon Mosier	1
12. Mike Bell	11	32. Jeff Matiasevich	1
13. Broc Glover	10	32. Steve Wise	1
14. Mike LaRocco	9	32. Pierre Karsmakers	1
15. Ron Lechien	8	32. Chuck Sun	1
15. Jimmy Ellis	8	32. Greg Albertyn	1
17. Jeff Emig	7	32. Rex Staten	1
17. Johnny O'Mara	7	32. Sebastien Tortelli	1
17. Chad Reed	7	32. Jaroslav Falta	1
17. David Vuillemin	7	32. Jim Pomeroy	1
21. Kevin Windham	6	32. Doug Dubach	1
22. Mike Kiedrowski	5	32. Nathan Ramsey	1
22. Kent Howerton	5	32. Rick Ryan	1

ALL-TIME AMA 500cc SUPERCROSS WIN LIST

1. Steve Stackable	2
1. Rich Eierstedt	2
2. Tim Hart	1
3. Gaylon Mosier	1
3. Roger DeCoster	1
3. Rex Staten	1
3. Gary Chaplin	1
3. Monte McCoy	1
3. Pat Ricter	1

1. Ricky Carmichael	26
2. Mark Barnett	25
3. Steve Lamson	21
4. James Stewart, Jr.	17
5. Guy Cooper	16
6. Broc Glover	14
7. Jeff Emig	13
7. George Holland	13
9. Jeff Ward	11
10. Ron Lechien	10
10. Mike Kiedrowski	10
11. Bob Hannah	8
11. Micky Dymond	8
11. Marty Smith	8
14. Doug Henry	7
14. Kevin Windham	7
14. Johnny O'Mara	7
14. Erik Kehoe	7
14. Travis Pastrana	7
19. Mike LaRocco	6
19. Mike Brown	6
21. Grant Langston	5
21. Robbie Reynard	5
21. Ryan Hughes	5
24. Stephane Roncada	4

24. Damon Bradshaw	4
24. Larry Ward	4
27. Jean-Michel Bayle	3
27. Damon Huffman	3
27. Danny LaPorte	3
27. Donny Schmit	3
31. Jeremy McGrath	2
31. John Dowd	2
31. Bryan Myerscough	2
31. Brock Sellards	2
31. Eddie Warren	2
31. Keith Bowen	2
31. Tim Hart	2
38. Chad Reed	1
38. Jim Ellis	1
38. Gaylon Mosier	1
38. Jeff Matiasevich	1
38. Steve Wise	1
38. Tim Ferry	1
38. A.J. Whiting	1
38. Brian Swink	1
38. Craig Anderson	1
38. Danny Smith	1
38. James Dobb	1

1. Ricky Carmichael		37	23. Donnie Hansen	3
2. Bob Hannah		27	23. Sebastien Tortelli	3
3. Rick Johnson		22	28. Broc Glover	2
4. Kent Howerton		18	28. Marty Smith	2
5. Jeff Emig		16	28. Johnny O'Mara	2
6. Jeremy McGrath		15	28. Jean-Michel Bayle	2
7. Jeff Ward		13	28. Gary Bailey	2
8. Jeff Stanton		12	28. Gunnar Lindstrom	2
8. Mike Kiedrowski		12	28. Sonny DeFeo	2
10. Mike LaRocco		11	35. Tim Hart	1
10. Gary Jones		11	35. Jeff Matiasevich	1
12. Kevin Windham		8	35. Steve Wise	1
13. Doug Henry		7	35. Tim Ferry	1
13. Pierre Karsmakers		7	35. Jim Pomeroy	1
13. Jim Weinert		7	35. Alan King	1
16. Ron Lechien		6	35. Bil Brossi	1
16. Damon Bradshaw		6	35. Billy Liles	1
16. John Dowd		6	35. Rick Thorwaldson	1
19. Jim Ellis		5	35. Bob Grossi	1
19. Tony DiStefano		5	35. Jimmy Button	1
19. Marty Tripes		5	35. John DeSoto	1
19. Greg Albertyn		5	35. Ken Zahrt	1
23. David Bailey		3	35. Kenny Keylon	1
23. Ezra Lusk		3	35. Michael Craig	1
23. David Vuillemin		3	35. Mickael Pichon	1

#	Name	Wins
1.	Broc Glover	19
2.	Pierre Karsmakers	16
3.	Brad Lackey	16
4.	David Bailey	15
5.	Jeff Ward	12
6.	Rick Johnson	11
7.	Jim Weinert	9
8.	Jeff Stanton	8
9.	Chuck Sun	7
10.	Mike Bell	6
10.	Rick Burgett	6
12.	Danny LaPorte	5
12.	Kent Howerton	5
14.	Jean-Michel Bayle	4
14.	Danny Chandler	4
16.	Mike Kiedrowski	3
16.	Darrell Shultz	3
16.	Gary Semics	3
16.	Goat Breker	3
16.	Michael Hartwig	3
21.	Ron Lechien	2
21.	Bob Hannah	2
21.	Marty Smith	2
21.	Mike LaRocco	2
21.	Gaylon Mosier	2
21.	Tony DiStefano	2
21.	Rex Staten	2
21.	Steve Stackable	2
21.	Barry Higgins	2
21.	Tommy Croft	2
32.	Marty Tripes	1
32.	Alan King	1
32.	Bill Grossi	1
32.	Rick Thorwaldson	1
32.	Bryan Kenney	1
32.	Denny Swartz	1
32.	Eric Eaton	1
32.	Wyman Priddy	1

*As of 1/2/04

Appendix B
Past Champions

AMA 250cc
SUPERCROSS CHAMPION

2004 - Chad Reed
2003 – Ricky Carmichael
2002 – Ricky Carmichael
2001 – Ricky Carmichael
2000 – Jeremy McGrath
1999 – Jeremy McGrath
1998 – Jeremy McGrath
1997 – Jeff Emig
1996 – Jeremy McGrath
1995 – Jeremy McGrath
1994 – Jeremy McGrath
1993 – Jeremy McGrath
1992 – Jeff Stanton
1991 – Jean-Michel Bayle
1990 – Jeff Stanton
1989 – Jeff Stanton
1988 – Rick Johnson
1987 – Jeff Ward
1986 – Rick Johnson
1985 – Jeff Ward
1984 – Johnny O'Mara
1983 – David Bailey
1982 – Donnie Hansen
1981 – Mark Barnett
1980 – Mike Bell
1979 – Bob Hannah
1978 – Bob Hannah
1977 – Bob Hannah
1976 – Jim Weinert
1975 – Jim Ellis
1974 – Pierre Karsmakers

A list of champions Team Pro Circuit has created over the years hangs on the entrance to its semi.
Ken Faught/Dirt Rider

McGrath at the Bercy Supercross in Paris, France, in 1996. Ken Faught/Dirt Rider

Jeff Emig, circa 1993, throws it sideways during a pre-season warm-up race in Perris, California. Ken Faught/Dirt Rider

James Stewart has the potential to raise the bar and forever alter the landscape of supercross and motocross. Ken Faught/Dirt Rider

AMA 125cc EASTERN REGION SUPERCROSS CHAMPION

2004 – James Stewart
2003 – Branden Jesseman
2002 – Chad Reed
2001 – Travis Pastrana
2000 – Stephane Roncada
1999 – Ernesto Fonseca
1998 – Ricky Carmichael
1997 – Tim Ferry
1996 – Mickael Pichon
1995 – Mickael Pichon
1994 – Ezra Lusk
1993 – Doug Henry
1992 – Brian Swink
1991 – Brian Swink
1990 – Denny Stephenson
1989 – Damon Bradshaw
1988 – Todd DeHoop
1987 – Ron Tichenor
1986 – Keith Turpin
1985 – Eddie Warren

AMA 125cc WESTERN REGION SUPERCROSS CHAMPION

2004 – Ivan Tedesco
2003 – James Stewart, Jr.
2002 – Travis Preston
2001 – Ernesto Fonseca
2000 – Shae Bentley
1999 – Nathan Ramsey
1998 – John Dowd
1997 – Kevin Windham
1996 – Kevin Windham
1995 – Damon Huffman
1994 – Damon Huffman
1993 – Jimmy Gaddis
1992 – Jeremy McGrath
1991 – Jeremy McGrath
1990 – Ty Davis
1989 – Jeff Matiasevich
1988 – Jeff Matiasevich
1987 – Willie Surratt
1986 – Donny Schmit
1985 – Bobby Moore

AMA 500cc NATIONAL MX CHAMPION

1993 – Mike LaRocco
1992 – Mike Kiedrowski
1991 – Jean-Michel Bayle
1990 – Jeff Ward
1989 – Jeff Ward
1988 – Rick Johnson
1987 – Rick Johnson
1986 – David Bailey
1985 – Broc Glover
1984 – David Bailey
1983 – Broc Glover
1982 – Darrell Shultz
1981 – Broc Glover
1980 – Chuck Sun
1979 – Danny LaPorte
1978 – Rick Burgett
1977 – Marty Smith
1976 – Kent Howerton
1975 – Jim Weinert
1974 – Jim Weinert
1973 – Pierre Karsmakers
1972 – Brad Lackey

125cc Western Region SX Champ John Dowd.
Ken Faught/Dirt Rider

AMA 125cc NATIONAL MOTOCROSS CHAMPION

2003 – Grant Langston
2002 – James Stewart, Jr.
2001 – Mike Brown
2000 – Travis Pastrana
1999 – Ricky Carmichael
1998 – Ricky Carmichael
1997 – Ricky Carmichael
1996 – Steve Lamson
1995 – Steve Lamson
1994 – Doug Henry
1993 – Doug Henry
1992 – Jeff Emig
1991 – Mike Kiedrowski
1990 – Guy Cooper
1989 – Mike Kiedrowski

1988 – George Holland
1987 – Micky Dymond
1986 – Micky Dymond
1985 – Ron Lechien
1984 – Jeff Ward
1983 – Johnny O'Mara
1982 – Mark Barnett
1981 – Mark Barnett
1980 – Mark Barnett
1979 – Broc Glover
1978 – Broc Glover
1977 – Broc Glover
1976 – Bob Hannah
1975 – Marty Smith
1974 – Marty Smith

Travis Pastrana won a 125cc National Championship, but never managed to win a single supercross.
Ken Faught/Dirt Rider

Ricky Carmichael whips it sideways during the 2000 Dallas supercross.
Ken Faught/Dirt Rider

AMA 250cc NATIONAL MX CHAMPION

2003 – Ricky Carmichael
2002 – Ricky Carmichael
2001 – Ricky Carmichael
2000 – Ricky Carmichael
1999 – Greg Albertyn
1998 – Doug Henry
1997 – Jeff Emig
1996 – Jeff Emig
1995 – Jeremy McGrath
1994 – Mike LaRocco
1993 – Mike Kiedrowski
1992 – Jeff Stanton
1991 – Jean-Michel Bayle
1990 – Jeff Stanton
1989 – Jeff Stanton
1988 – Jeff Ward

1987 – Rick Johnson
1986 – Rick Johnson
1985 – Jeff Ward
1984 – Rick Johnson
1983 – David Bailey
1982 – Donnie Hansen
1981 – Kent Howerton
1980 – Kent Howerton
1979 – Bob Hannah
1978 – Bob Hannah
1977 – Tony DiStefano
1976 – Tony DiStefano
1975 –Tony DiStefano
1974 – Gary Jones
1973 – Gary Jones
1972 – Gary Jones

Index